> # *"...I mean to prepare the way for futurity."*
>
> ## –Alexander Hamilton
>
> Age 12 (or 14) in a letter to Ned Stevens
> November 11, 1769

DESTINED TO BE A
HAMILTON

True Life Stories of **Mary Anne Hamilton**,
Great-Great Granddaughter-in-Law of
Founding Father **Alexander Hamilton**

BY
MARY ANNE HAMILTON

WITH
HELENA REYNOLDS

DEDICATION

This book is dedicated to the memory of my dear friend, **Rand Scholet**, founder, and former president of the *Alexander Hamilton Awareness Society*. Rand's big heart, booming voice, and boundless enthusiasm for *All Things Hamilton* were unforgettable. He enriched my life with his friendship and generosity. He inspired me to continue promoting the Hamilton Family Legacy that my late husband, Laurens Morgan Hamilton, passionately tried to publicize. And the educational journey we embarked upon together gave me a whole new lease on life in my 80s. I'll forever be grateful to my friend, Rand.

TABLE OF CONTENTS

INTRODUCTION

"I believe I was destined to be a Hamilton for a very special reason."

–Mary Anne Hamilton

Jorge, please get the letter that arrived today."

My neighbors Vince Post and Jorge Arroyo met nightly with me on their patio to enjoy drinks and the Florida breeze. On this cool September evening in 2015, we were all pretty laid-back, making small talk as usual.

Footsteps sounded as Jorge returned with an envelope in his hand. "This one?" He held it up.

Taking a sip of his scotch, Vince nodded. "Yes, that's it." He took it, casually opened the flap, and pulled out tickets for a Broadway theater show in New York.

Vince often surprised Jorge, his longtime partner, with a trip to New York or even Europe. I thought *How nice, the fellas are going to see another show.*

But instead of only two tickets, Vince held three and looked right at me. "I've been reading in the *New York Times* about a show on Broadway called *Hamilton, An American Musical.* From what I can tell, it's a story about Founding Father Alexander Hamilton and, since you're related to him by marriage, I thought you might like to see it with us. Some of the music is rap and hip-hop."

Rap and hip-hop? That made me think of kids with blaring bass beats, booming their swaying cars by my house. I knew nothing about the show, but I trusted Vince's judgment. If he thought I'd like it, I probably would. But his offer posed a massive dilemma for me:

I hate shopping. What am I going to wear in New York?

I looked up reviews about the show online, which were mostly positive. I also learned that the musical involved many types of music in addition to rap and hip-hop, and that the historical lyrics focused on my late husband's great-great-grandfather.

As I read more, I was definitely interested, but my inclinations were overshadowed by my dismay of having nothing appropriate to wear for a trip to a Broadway theater in New York City.

Vince had spent about six weeks searching online for the right tickets and prices for a performance the following spring. He chose a confirmed evening when the show's creator, Lin-Manuel Miranda, was playing the lead role.

One night, while Vince was online, previously unavailable tickets suddenly and magically opened up. Center section, third row! Three tickets for only $352 each! Later, he wished he'd bought more. The going rate for similar tickets in the first three rows was $2,000 to $3,000 each on April 11, 2016, the night of our show.

My late husband had been an avid promoter of Alexander Hamilton's legacy, but I was too busy working and raising my five children to pay much attention. Never mind that the Founding Father was *my* great-great-grandfather-in-law.

I didn't think I had time for history, and at first, I didn't really care. But that began to change when I watched my soon-to-be-husband meet Queen Elizabeth II on a dock on a West Indies island a few months before we got married. It was spectacular. The people who greeted us so graciously on Nevis sparked an interest in me to learn about history. I became intrigued…sort of. But not enough to read books about the past. Life events—and raising five children—kept that history spark from becoming a flame.

My daughter-in-law, Jackie Clark, and my two granddaughters, Lisa and Alyssa, took me shopping one day; it turned out to be an enjoyable spectacle.

"Try this one on, Grandma." They searched the racks and I felt like a model, waiting to try on whatever garment meandered my way from the other side of the dressing room curtain. We found a beautiful dress that fit, so I could relax a bit when thinking about the trip.

It seemed almost providential. My neighbors had invited me to see a musical production based on the history of my late husband's ancestors. Little did I know how the focus of my life would change a mere seven months later at a Broadway theater in New York City.

———◆———

That 2016 musical extravaganza at the *Richard Rodgers Theatre* in New York was a long way from the Gramercy Inn Cocktail Lounge in Washington, DC, where I worked in 1965. Back then, I was a 31-year-old struggling waitress and soon-to-be single mother of five.

One night, I served the hotel owner, the manager, and an older gentleman with them. After the elderly man tipped me a $50 bill and left—in his fancy Lincoln Continental with a full-time driver—the owner and manager seemed upset that I didn't appear to be star-struck.

They both were astounded. "Do you know who that man is?"

"No, but I like his tip," I grinned. $50 then is like $500 now so it was very impressive.

"He is Alexander Hamilton's great-great-grandson and J. P. Morgan's grandson."

My blank face showed my indifference. *So what?* I knew Mr. Hamilton was on the ten-dollar bill, but I had no idea who Mr. Morgan was. I didn't have time for history. I had a job to do and five kids to care for. Plus, I had served many famous people over the years so I wasn't impressed.

Back in the mid-1950s, one of my well-known patrons was controversial Vice President Richard Nixon, enjoying a Saturday evening out with a group of friends and colleagues. I might have caused a mini controversy myself when the partiers were drinking and dancing past midnight. At the time, a Blue Law was in effect, prohibiting drinking alcohol on Sundays. So even though they were on the dance floor, I removed all their drinks.

I thought to myself *The law is the law, right?*

Wrong.

The head captain, George, was upset with me and put their drinks back before they returned. I could have caused a historical controversy involving the US vice president and his friends had I pushed for that Blue Law enforcement.

Historical events and cultural controversies have played a huge role in my life over the years. Some may call them coincidences and others might label them destiny markers, but they began early. Before I was 10 years old, my family moved to East *Schuyler* Road in Silver Spring, Maryland. At the Shoreham Hotel's Palladian Room, my waitress uniform was a *colonial styled costume* similar to period attire worn by our nation's founding mothers and daughters in the late 1700s. And later, I worked as a cocktail waitress at the *Hamilton Hotel*. I didn't know it then, but these three occurrences may have been glimpses of my destiny.

How?

Alexander *Hamilton* was—and to some, still is—a controversial Founding Father. Like all of us, he had human faults, but unlike most of us, he had super human brilliance and vision. During *colonial* days, Alexander, and his wife, Elizabeth *Schuyler* Hamilton, helped create the foundation that produced the beginning of the Great American Experiment, also known as the United States of America.

Whether by coincidence or not, my life was impacted by these and other events that appeared to have led me down a specific pathway, destined to marry into Alexander and Elizabeth Hamilton's family. And it was a long and narrow, winding, and often extremely bumpy road.

You may notice a detour or two, but don't let them distract you from my main memoir message: *I believe I was destined to be a Hamilton for a very special reason.* I've inserted three features called *Laurens' Lists A, B, and C,* which reveal facts about Alexander Hamilton's life, education, military efforts, and nation-building contributions. In my opinion, these truths are as valuable as my life stories, if not more so.

My journal entries, letters, articles, and anecdotal stories are noted in sections. I've inserted photos next to descriptive narratives. Three appendices provide links to additional information, historical details, and memorable stories. Also included are Quick Response (QR) Codes to online video clips of my speeches and other relevant resources.

So, fasten your seatbelt. I truly hope you enjoy my Hamilton *Life Stories* educational ride.

CHAPTER 1
DESTINATION: NEW YORK

My Life's Mystery Unveiled
Via the Arts

The handsome young man greeted us graciously as he entered the dressing room where we'd been told to wait for him. After our introductions, I told the youthful author, "I tried to buy your new book yesterday but they didn't have it."

His brows furrowed. "I'm sorry, it doesn't release until tomorrow." A gleam arose in his eyes. Raising his index finger, he quipped, "Just a sec, I'll be right back."

He returned with a brand-new, yet-to-be-released book in his hands.

The date was April 11, 2016.

The dressing room was backstage in the Richard Rodgers Theatre in New York City.

My name is Mary Anne Hamilton. My late husband was Laurens Morgan Hamilton, a descendant of America's Founding Father Alexander Hamilton and global financier J. P. Morgan.

The young author was Lin-Manuel Miranda, creator, composer, and original star of Broadway's mega-hit entitled *Hamilton, An American Musical,* which is based on my late husband's great-great-grandfather's lifetime contributions and accomplishments.

The book was *Hamilton: The Revolution,* lyrics, photographs, and informative notes, by Lin-Manuel Miranda and his friend, Jeremy McCarter.

Lin-Manuel Miranda posed with me after my neighbors Vince and Jorge took me to see *Hamilton, An American Musical* in New York on April 11, 2016.
Photo by Jorge Arroyo, Courtesy of Mary Anne Hamilton

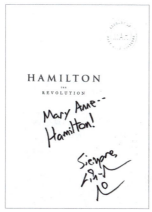

Lin-Manuel Miranda signed his book for me. He also signed my show playbill.

Not only did Mr. Miranda give me his first edition copy of the book, but he also personally autographed it to me, signed my playbill, and even posed with me for a photograph. It was a wonderful evening that eventually marked the start of a new era in my life.

The events that led up to that night were exciting as well. Vince and Jorge had planned a wonderful trip of sightseeing in New York and I kept an ongoing record.

My Journal: We flew to Kennedy Airport in New York on Saturday, April 9, 2016. A limousine was waiting to take us to the *French Quarters Hotel* on West 46th Street, a block from the theater. Our two-bedroom suite was very luxurious. Vince had ordered a beautiful flower bouquet that made the living room especially welcoming.

On Sunday morning, we climbed the *Statue of Liberty.* That is, Vince and Jorge walked up to the crown of Lady Liberty, but I took the elevator. At the age of 82, I knew I wouldn't make it up that far.

The Hamilton Grange has been moved twice but still sits on land originally owned by Hamilton. Today it is known as Hamilton Grange National Memorial.

We then stopped at *The Hamilton Grange*, the only home Alexander Hamilton helped design and had built for his family. Unfortunately, we were rushed by an impatient host, but we were able to tour most of the three levels of this exclusive, historical mansion.

The following day we visited *Trinity Church* where Alexander Hamilton and his wife, Eliza, were buried. We were met by marketing director, Lynn Goswick, who showed us around the church and graveyard. She then escorted us across Wall Street to the Episcopal Church headquarters.

Anne, the archivist at Trinity, had put together a table full of articles signed by Alexander Hamilton, including rent receipts for their church pew, baptism papers for his children, and legal counsel documents.

They presented me with a wonderful book, entitled *Trinity Near and Far, Now and Then*. It was the history of Trinity Church going back to the 1600s.

The Trinity Church archivist showed me the Hamilton family's church pew registration.

That night, we walked through a light drizzle to the Richard Rodgers Theatre to experience *Hamilton, An American Musical*, live and in person.

Our hotel was only a block away from the Richard Rodgers Theatre, so we walked.

I had written to tell Lin-Manuel Miranda that we were going to be attending his show that evening. When we arrived, we spoke with the attendant who ushered us to our seats. He told us to remain there after the show and someone would come and get us.

The musical was more than wonderful, and as I watched, it became clear. *Now I see why Laurens was so passionate about Hamilton.* The production was overwhelming with history, singing, dancing, lights, action, a moving staircase on a revolving floor, and more history. Laurens would have loved it because it told his great-great-grandfather's stories using the arts to engage with the audience, thus, producing a thought-provoking experience.

After the show we remained in our seats. Watching people. Waiting for our escort. Anxious to meet the cast.

One odd observation involved a person bringing what appeared to be a reading lamp on a single pole that was plugged in and set near the edge of the stage. Vince called it a "ghost light," a theater custom to keep the stage 'spirits' happy after everyone is gone.

Finally, we were escorted onto the stage...with about 30 other people. Vince spoke to the person in charge and told her I was Alexander Hamilton's great-great-granddaughter-in-law. She beckoned to the three of us. We followed her backstage to a dressing room, and what happened next was, and sometimes still is, so surreal that it was shared as my opening story of this chapter.

14

Elizabeth Hamilton posed for this portrait by artist Ralph Earl while he was in debtor's prison. Alexander's portrait was painted by John Trumbull.

The next day, at the *Museum of the City of New York*, we saw original paintings of Alexander and Elizabeth Hamilton. Her portrait had been donated by my sister-in-law, Mrs. Alexander (Morgan) Hamilton and my brother-in-law, Pierpont Morgan Hamilton, an Air Force Major General and a WWII *Congressional Medal of Honor* recipient.

After we returned home, Andrew Meacham, a former staff reporter with the *Tampa Bay Times*, wrote an article about me and our trip to New York. The following excerpt from his piece captured my experience well:

"As the lights came up at the Richard Rodgers Theatre in New York, Aaron Burr was rapping ruminations about his rival, Alexander Hamilton.

Mary Anne Hamilton watched from the center of the third row. Fans of Hamilton, the hottest Broadway musical in decades with a record 16 Tony nominations, are desperate for seats. Everyone wants to be in; it seems impossible to get in.

And yet, there was this retired real estate agent from Seminole, FL. At age 82, she was the last person who ever expected to go. She thought rap was something teenagers blared driving past her house. She had never seen a Broadway show. She never would have cared about Alexander Hamilton, but for this fact:

Her late husband was his great-great-grandson.

Mary Anne always called herself 'a trophy wife.' For decades, she had no time for history. She had lived with money and without, near stature and yet far from glamour. Strung together, it had led her here.

In a way, this performance was one final benefit from her marriage. One more gift she never really asked for." (See QR Code p. 208.)

(By Andrew Meacham, *Tampa Bay Times*, May 28, 2016 – Used with permission)

Mr. Meacham's article mentions a *gift I never really asked for.* That phrase could describe my entire life. My journal notes about our great trip to New York spanned a short six days during my 82nd year of life. But my memory journals of my first 81 years are seared into my mind. The earliest of these memories, *the many gifts I never really asked for*, are shared over the next several chapters.

CHAPTER 2
RETROSPECTIVE DESTINATIONS

*My Youth-to-Marriage
Memory Lane*

One day, my little sister was so excited she could barely breathe. "I have a new friend who lives on a beautiful farm and she invited us to come over to ride ponies with her. Do you want to go?" We were both attending a new Catholic middle school in the mid-1940s, so meeting new friends and having exciting adventures were quite a thrill.

"Of course I do," I exclaimed. That invitation sparked my life-long love of horses and riding. We spent many days playing pretend war games and racing around their gigantic meadows. In no time we were jumping horses, going to horse shows, and riding in fox hunts.

At age 14, my favorite horse to ride and jump in competitions was Blue Mist.

Horseback riding added to my fond, early-childhood recollections of walking to a local Catholic school, going to the library, attending the movies, swimming in Chesapeake Bay, vacationing at Ocean City, Maryland, and going to Mass every Sunday.

Although my dad's loyalties were to the North and Mother's were to the South, my parents Raymond and Nelia Eichhorn provided a wonderful loving home for our family. My two sisters and I had an older brother and I was the middle daughter, born during a Washington, DC blizzard on Sunday, February 4, 1934.

I was named Mary after my grandmother, Mary Smith, who had also been born on February 4, 1875. In addition to me, her elder son, my Uncle Edward, had been born on February 4, 1900, as well. The date February 4 provides an unusual coincidence in our family.

My parents told us as children, "When you make your bed, you have to lie in it." I grew up knowing that anything I chose to do, I had to live with the consequences. They meant it when they stated, "Don't come back home crying. You made the choice, now you have to live with it."

I was very laid-back and easy-going as a young girl. I did what I was told and thus, I was never spanked. Ever. But combined with my naivete, such inclinations made me very vulnerable.

In 1943, we moved from DC to Silver Spring, Maryland, where I attended 5th grade in a public school while waiting to enroll at St. Michael's Catholic School. As mentioned, that's where my little sister met the family who invited us to ride horses. Our new hobby provided great memories, but it also created challenges for our entire family. And some were life-impacting encounters.

Due to unfortunate circumstances, which I'll share more about later, I had to move temporarily to a place where, among other things, I learned to type nearly 80 words a minute. I also had to participate in a painful legal procedure that many thought was sensational enough for the press to cover. I was only 15 years old. The newspapers dramatized the vivid stories of my plight, so when school started, some students bullied me.

One boy in my new school came to my defense. "Leave her alone!" he shouted as he hauled off and hit the guy who'd been bullying me, knocking him like a rag doll across the lunch table. He hobbled away muttering.

"Thanks," I gushed. *My new hero.* I thought I'd found my savior. "What's your name?"

"Leo," he beamed. "Where's your next class? I'll walk with you." He didn't leave my side until we got to my classroom.

The bullies left me alone after that.

As we walked and talked that first time, and many subsequent days, I discovered that Leo was a senior, a year ahead of me in school. He was taking boxing lessons, which was why he could defend me. We became inseparable.

Leo worked after school at the Statler Hotel as a guest attendant, buying theater and airline tickets for patrons. He was very committed to the hotel. In fact, he ended up working at the same hotel—which eventually became the Statler Hilton—for the next 50 years.

When my senior year started, I discovered I was pregnant so I quit school and Leo and I were married on October 14, 1950. I was only 16. We moved in to his parents' home in Arlington, Virginia.

Because I was able to type extremely well, I got my first job as a clerk-typist at the Pentagon. Thus, I was a pregnant teenager as well as a government worker until May, 1951.

Saturday, June 2, 1951 was supposed to be the day of my high school graduation, but instead it was the day that our first son, Leo, Jr. was born. We moved into a basement apartment of a home in nearby Maryland. A few months later, I discovered I was pregnant again.

An apartment complex had an opening so we moved there before our second son, Michael, was born in July, 1952. I stayed home with the boys. By then, Leo, Sr. was promoted to bell hop at the Statler. His schedule alternated between working days one week and then working nights the next. Money was tight. I started looking for an evening job that would allow me to care for the boys during the daytime until Leo got home from his hotel shift.

I got a job selling baked goods at a local drive-in restaurant/bakery called the Hot Shoppe on Rhode Island Avenue. Swing shift: 5 to 11 p.m. It didn't seem fair that the waitresses could leave at 11 p.m. with pockets full of tip money, but I had to stay another 30 minutes, putting the baked goods away and counting the shop's money from the till. After two weeks, I asked to be a dining room waitress. At first they denied my request, but they relented when I threatened to go to another Hot Shoppe.

My section was inside but when the curb boys got busy on the weekends, my boss assigned me to be outside where I waited on patrons while they sat in their cars. Many were teenagers like me, so sometimes, it took a long time for them to decide what to order.

I was patient. Often, I chatted with them while waiting for their orders. Once they discovered I was married with two little boys, many teenaged customers began tipping me exceptionally well.

Finally, I got to work as a counter waitress inside. When the two regular staff had their two nights off, I covered all four of their shifts. My tip totals increased even more because patrons seated at the counter stools came and went quickly. And they were big tippers.

In 1954, shortly after turning 20, I discovered I was pregnant again. I quit working and our daughter Kitty was born in November. Caring for three children under the age of three was quite a challenge. So were our financial issues.

A hostess at the Hot Shoppe, my former workplace, became manager of the Neptune Room on 14th Street in downtown DC. She offered me a job as a night waitress from 5 p.m. to 2 a.m. When I turned 21, I was then able to serve drinks, and tip totals were even higher.

After a few months, however, Leo didn't like me working so late downtown so he got me a job working the dinner hours and the Sunday breakfast shift at the Statler Hotel.

I joined the hotel union, but after about a month, union regulations forced the evening waitresses to quit serving breakfasts. That was fine with me. It was too early and the breakfast guests didn't tip very well. The union found me other assignments, working banquets until a full-time job opened up.

In the fall of 1955, I began working at the Shoreham Hotel cafeteria from 5 to 10 p.m. One of my patrons was Mr. Alfred, the head waiter of Shoreham's newly opened dining and dancing pavilion named the Palladian Room. I asked if he could help me transfer to his staff. Within a week, I was assigned to the elegant Colonial Williamsburg-type Palladian Room, where we waitresses wore long dresses with lacy pinafores and ruffled caps, similar to authentic clothing of America's colonial times.

The waiters wore knee britches and buckled shoes. We served hors d'oeuvres from narrow carts resembling mini-Ferris wheels and ladled soup from rolling wagons.

Our head captain, George, and I served soup at the Palladian Room.

Dinner was delivered on wagons with roast beef sliced at each table. The bartenders mixed our customers' drinks at a table-side bar wagon. About 9:30 p.m., the wagons were cleared away. The dance band played until 2 a.m., except for Saturday nights, when we closed at midnight due to the Blue Law mentioned earlier.

Another law was imposed on our family after our fourth child, Anna, was born in February, 1957. We got evicted…kicked out into the cold. Apartment *laws* prohibited families with four children from renting two-bedroom units. Fortunately, we found a house we could 'rent-to-own' while applying for an FHA loan. It needed a bookcase as a second-floor staircase protective barrier. We built the bookcase, the house passed the appraisal and inspection, and we closed on our very first home. Our mortgage was $15,500 for our College Park house.

In 1959, I became a cocktail waitress in the posh Purple Tree Cocktail Lounge at the Hamilton Hotel downtown. I served only drinks and really appreciated the music provided by a lovely lady on the piano every evening.

Our fifth child, John, was born in October, 1961. The next year I went to work at the cocktail lounge in

I enjoyed the pianist at the Purple Tree Cocktail Lounge

the Windsor Park Hotel. We served many celebrities, politicians, and professional athletes, including the Washington Senators and the Washington Redskins, who stayed in our hotel so their coaches could check on them when they played in town. They frequented our cocktail lounge for late-night drinks.

One night, a couple of baseball guys, who had both been New York Yankees, stayed until the wee hours of the morning catching up, since one of them had become a pitcher for the Washington Senators.

The next day, their teams had a double header against each other. When they came back the following night, they told me that one of them won the first game and the other won the nightcap. In spite of getting very little sleep, they both had won their games.

The Washington Senators stayed for 6-8 weeks, so I got to know the baseball players fairly well. The hotel owner provided this special end-of-the season cake.

One evening, Don Zimmer, a Senators player, and some of the guys wanted to go to the races in Virginia. They needed wheels, so Don came to me. "Say, Mary Anne, can we borrow your car to go to the horse races?"

"Sure." I gave him the keys and two dollars. "Win something for me, bet on number four in the first race after you get there."

When they got back, they moaned to me, "Poor Mary Anne's horse, came in last…poor Mary Anne's horse, came in last…." As they continued whining, one of the guys pulled out a money roll and began peeling 10-and 20-dollar bills off the stack. They gave me $120, but I doubt it was from any race winnings. It was probably to say thanks for the use of my car.

Nice guys.

In 1964, my partner, Betty, and I were asked to help open the Gramercy Inn Cocktail Lounge, across from Scott Circle. We designed our own uniforms: gold or red mini dresses with white ruffled trim on the puffed sleeves and scooped necklines, little white aprons, and fishnet stockings…like a 'French upstairs maid' costume.

The Gramercy Inn Cocktail Lounge opened in May, 1964 and things went exceptionally well with our new endeavors.

Unfortunately, things were not going very well with our marriage. Because of many reasons, Leo and I had grown apart. We were only 30 and 33 and we already had five children under the age of 13. It was extremely stressful for all of us.

In the summer of 1964, we realized it would be best for us to split up, so Leo moved out and we filed for divorce. In Maryland, the relevant divorce laws required an 18-month waiting period if children were involved.

I continued to work during the evenings and Leo came to our home to care for the children after his shift. Because he worked evenings every other week, I arranged a room-and-board trade with a college student to help fill in the gaps, but that didn't always work out. Our oldest sons were 12 and 13, and our youngest was only three years old. The girls were six and nine. Fortunately, neighbors helped when needed.

It was an extremely difficult time in my life. Sometimes Leo got caught in traffic and was late. In the meantime, if a neighbor was not around to care for the children, then I was late, too.

At times I got frustrated. But I had already conquered so many challenges, I knew I'd be able to find a way to overcome this one… somehow….

CHAPTER 3
DESTINED TO WAIT

*My Waitressing Work and
Waiting for My Divorce*

In 1965, my life became a world of *wait*ing: *wait*ing on customers as a *wait*ress and *wait*ing 18 months for my divorce to become final. I continued working at the Gramercy Inn Cocktail Lounge nearly every evening, and Leo faithfully came every other week after work to care for our children. It was difficult at times, but we made it work.

As mentioned in the introduction, one night in early November, 1965, I served the hotel owner, the manager, and an older gentleman who walked with a cane. I was not particularly impressed by him but his $50 tip definitely got my attention. Even when they told me he was Laurens Morgan Hamilton—Alexander Hamilton's great-great-grandson and J. P. Morgan's grandson—I felt indifferent. I thought of him as just another one of my many evening patrons. I tried to give all of my customers VIP service, regardless of their historical or celebrity status.

I truly didn't have time for history, so their name-dropping meant nothing. My focus was on my job serving customers, and my five children I had to care and provide for.

The following evening was my day off. Imagine my surprise—and immediate disdain—when I returned to work and my coworkers and regular customers all told me the same story.

"Hey, Mary Anne," they teased. "That old guy, Hamilton, came in yesterday on your day off and announced to everyone that he's going to marry you."

"He did what?" I was aghast. "How could he say that when we've barely talked and haven't even gone on a single date?"

Plus, I thought to myself, *I still have three more months to wait until my divorce is final.*

My regular patrons and coworkers were smiling with amusement. "Don't shoot the messengers, we're just telling you what we heard him say."

I'd heard his name and status from my supervisors after our initial encounter, but I still had no idea who he really was, where he came from, or why he was sitting with our hotel owner and restaurant manager. There was no way I could have known that he had grown up in his family's English Gothic style, four-story mansion with 52 rooms, 32 bedrooms, and 20 bathrooms. During the time that his family lived there—1904 to 1939—the 2,000-acre, opulent complex in Tuxedo, New York, was known as Table Rock Estates.

It was also impossible for me to have known that the old man—who walked with a cane and announced he was going to marry me—was the son of Juliet Morgan Hamilton, whose father, global financier J. P. Morgan, had built the Table Rock Estates for her.

There had been no indication that the old man—who told my customers he was going to marry me before he asked me—had attended Groton School in Massachusetts, one of the nation's best boarding schools. He had volunteered to join the Army in 1918, and had served as a second lieutenant in World War I before returning to New York in 1920.

I also had no way to know that the old man—who told my coworkers he was going to marry me before he asked me—already had three ex-wives and his divorce from wife #4 was not yet finalized. Because neither of us were officially divorced, his marriage declaration was even more preposterous. And the fact that he was 65 while I was only 31 meant that he was a whopping 34 years older than me. Incredibly, he was only two years younger than my own mother.

I was so focused on my job and my children that I hadn't even considered another relationship, let alone a new marriage. Nope. That was the furthest thing from my mind. Because Leo and I had married when I was only 16, I had never really dated, or been courted, or known what it might be like to be proposed to in the old-fashioned way. Plus, my lawyer said not to date for 18 months or Leo could have grounds to take the children.

In the midst of my thoughts about the absurdity of the old man's announcement, I suddenly realized that not only did I know nothing about him, but he probably knew nothing about me. *That's it!* That's how I could dissuade him…just spell everything out for him the next time he's at the Gramercy Inn during my shift. Once he finds out, he'll retract his marriage declaration as fast as he blurted it out on my day off. It might be fun to watch him back-pedal—like most of the other guys had done—after hearing about my large, young family.

The next evening, my coworker leaned over the bar and nodded slightly to the door. "There he is," she whispered. She'd been there on my day off when the old man had made his marital declaration to my coworkers and our patrons.

I glanced up nonchalantly but lowered my gaze quickly to avoid making eye contact. I didn't even know him and I was appalled by what he did. At least, what *they said* he did.

Doubts crept in. *What if they were all playing a joke on me?* As I looked up, that thought disappeared when he smiled and began walking towards me, tapping his cane lightly with every other step. His suit and tie were impeccable and he carried an air of confidence. Warmth and kindness projected from his eyes. Nice old man... he appeared to be a very nice, older gentleman.

My mind was reeling. Thoughts were racing between *what if he said it and really meant it...this is so unreal,* and *the audacity of the man...the sooner I set him straight, the better.*

As he approached the bar, my memory of his generous tip only two nights before, triggered my conscience. *He gave you a $50 tip, the least you can do is be cordial to him.*

"Hello Mary Anne." He extended his right hand, smiling warmly. *Such a gentleman.*

"Hi." I grinned at him and gingerly placed my hand on his. He shook my hand briefly, but firmly.

"Laurens, Laurens Hamilton." He didn't seem the least bit chagrined that I seemed to have forgotten his name.

"Hello Mr. Hamilton, may I get you a drink?" This was a cocktail lounge and I was a waitress, so it was the least I could do.

He hooked his cane on the back of a chair in my section and sat down. "Yes, please, scotch and water. Thank you."

As I turned the corner to order his beverage from the bartender, I heard the hotel owner's voice. "Hello, Laurens, so good to see you. Please join us at our table."

"Thank you," was all I heard, followed by hushed whispers I couldn't decipher.

When I returned with his drink, I was surprised to see him still seated at my table. "I have a question for you, Mary Anne." His kind eyes were twinkling.

I glanced around, relieved to see that all the patrons and my coworkers were engaged with their tasks or guests at hand.

"Okaaay…." I tried not to panic.

He smiled again and I was taken aback by his gentle manner. "On your next evening off, would you be so kind as to join me for dinner?"

There it was. My chance to drop my family status bomb and watch the fallout with amusement.

"I don't know," I hesitated. "I'm pretty busy on my days off. You see, I'm a single mother working evenings because I have five children to care and provide for, and my divorce isn't yet finalized…."

There, I did it. I expected him to say something abrupt, like 'thanks for the drink, I'll take my check, please,' as some of the previous guys had said. Or pull out his own family pictures to share with me, as other men had done.

But he did neither. He was still there, seated at my table, smiling. "How old are your children?"

Hmmm…the number of kids didn't seem to repel him but I'll bet their ages will.

"Two boys, 14 and 13; two girls, 10 and 7, and a 4-year-old little boy."

I still expected him to make an unceremonious exit, but he kept smiling.

His next statements blew me away. "Oh, so you have three boys and two girls. I'd really like to meet them."

My jaw dropped. "You would?"

"Yes, I'd love to meet your children. What are their names?"

I was in such a state of shock, I nearly forgot their names. "Uhh…Leo, Mike, Kitty, Anna and John." I listed them all, surprised that he seemed to be interested.

He smiled and sipped his drink slowly, appearing to absorb my kids' names and ages. I excused myself for a moment to give another customer his check. When I returned, I finally stammered, "Ahhh… about your dinner invitation, it's really nice of you, but is it okay if I think about it?"

He seemed happy that I didn't say no. "Oh sure, sure…take your time. I have to be away on business but I'll be back next week." He finished his drink.

I smiled, relieved. "Okay, I'll see you then. Thank you."

He arose, slipped another large bill on the table, smiled at me again, picked up his cane, and left.

Suddenly, I realized what his hushed conversation must have been with the hotel owner. He didn't want to move to the owner's table because he wanted privacy to ask me on a real date.

For all practical purposes, I should have said no. But the events of the past three days were so overwhelming for me that 'practicality' went by the wayside. Now I had the entire weekend to think of reasons—in addition to my lawyer's warning—that I should say no.

But what if I said *yes*?

CHAPTER 4
COURTSHIP PREDESTINED

*Gifts and Trips from an
Elderly Patron*

When Mr. Hamilton came in the following week, I'd made up my mind. If he asked me out again, I would go if it was during daytime hours. I was curious about his intentions so getting to know him might give me a glimpse of who he really was. At the time, he was merely an elderly acquaintance… and my lawyer didn't say I couldn't have friends.

He seemed to be such a gentleman, and he was extremely generous, as demonstrated by his $50 tip. But the next week, he had a different question after the hostess seated him in my section.

"Hello Mary Anne. When's your next break?" He smiled.

What a thoughtful person. He obviously wanted to speak with me but he attempted to avoid interrupting me during my work hours. "In about 20 minutes."

"May we speak then or should I wait until after your shift?"

Such a considerate man. Maybe I misjudged him. "During my break."

He nodded. "I'll be right here."

At break time, Mr. Hamilton asked again if I would join him for dinner.

"Is it okay if we do lunch?" I countered. "I like to spend my few evenings off with my children."

"Of course," he grinned. "I'm in the Hamilton Suite at the Madison Hotel. My driver can pick you up Thursday at 12 noon if you give me your address…"

"Thanks, but I'll drive myself." I knew that the Madison was just a few blocks from the Gramercy Inn.

The following Thursday, still a bit apprehensive, I drove to the hotel. If needed, I wanted to be able to get away in my car. At least it would be daylight if our lunch get-together went sideways.

I found the Hamilton Suite and knocked softly. An older lady opened the door. "Hi there, you must be Mary Anne." She smiled, "I'm Mrs. Burns, please come in."

Mr. Hamilton arose from the far side of the lavish suite. "Hello, my dear. I'm so glad you've come. You've met my nurse, Mrs. Burns, and this is my driver, Chief."

"Hello…" As I smiled at them, two lively poodles interrupted us, bouncing around Mr. Hamilton's ankles. "This is Bruno and his daughter, Dolly Madison."

I bent down to pet them both. "They're adorable."

As I arose, he graciously introduced me. "This is my friend, Mary Anne. Come, let me show you around." Mrs. Burns took my coat and disappeared around the corner with Chief. The poodles retreated to the sofa.

Chaperones! I relaxed immediately and marveled at the exquisite décor, especially one portrait on the wall.

He pointed to the elegant painting of a gentleman in a vintage military uniform, "This is my great-great-grandfather, Alexander Hamilton, our most significant Founding Father, in my opinion. In fact, this suite is named for him."

I was impressed. We then moved to the dining room table and enjoyed a delicious lunch. Mr. Hamilton proved to be as much of a gentleman as he'd been during our prior meetings.

Many invitations were extended and accepted during the following weeks. At no time was he inappropriate, which could be expected with Mrs. Burns, Chief and the delightful poodles on the premises. But, even in the back seat of the Lincoln, when we were alone during an evening out, he never tried to grope me or kiss me or even hold my hand. Not once.

What a gentleman he is, I thought. *So old-fashioned... that must be the way his parents raised him.*

Later, I discovered another reason.

———◆———

Mr. Hamilton also followed through on his marital declaration he'd made during my day off. On November 16, 1965, only twelve days after we met, he started a letter to my mother with the following paragraph:

"My dear Mrs. O'Reilly,

Not having yet the pleasure of meeting you, I, nevertheless, have two good reasons at least for feeling like I know you. I have seen a photo of you and I have met your daughter, Mary Anne. Not to beat around the bush, it is definitely the latter who is the motivating cause behind this letter. As her mother, it is natural that you should be curious as to my intentions and my interest so far as Mary Anne is concerned. I am happy to be able to anticipate any such question by assuring you that my intentions are strictly honorable and my interest definitely matrimonial...."

I couldn't believe it when Mother read me his letter. Not only did he announce to my coworkers and customers that he planned to marry me, but he even told my mother before he told me!

He also followed through on his desire to meet my children. In fact, a mere three weeks after we met, he arranged for all of us to join him for Thanksgiving dinner and an overnight stay at the Holiday Inn in Virginia. He was extremely kind to the children and showed a genuine interest in all of them.

Thanksgiving, 1965. L-R: Leo Jr., John, Mike, Laurens, Bruno (poodle), me, Anna, Kitty

Laurens showered me with jewelry—a set of diamond earrings, two brooches with diamonds and emeralds. I'd never had such glamorous jewelry and wearing it made me nervous. (Especially after I lost a piece worth $2,000 and we had to file an insurance claim.)

To top things off, Laurens had an auto dealership order my family a brand-new station wagon. I kept the jewelry but made him cancel the car order. It seemed like too much. I had just bought a brand-new Pontiac for our family so we had a new car. (I still had a loan balance but I didn't tell him.)

Laurens invited me to the racetrack for the International Races in Baltimore, and to lunch and dinner at his Madison Hotel penthouse. He was a total gentleman everywhere we went and he made me feel very special.

In fact, as unreal as it may sound, he even offered to pay me an amount equal to my wages and tips so I could stay home and care for my five children until my divorce was finalized!

Overwhelmed. That's how I felt.

Between working nights in a high-end cocktail lounge, taking care of five children, being wined and dined in the finest places, and receiving an unusual offer of a 'stipend to stay home' that any working single mom would covet, I was totally stunned by his unbelievable offer.

I was more than overwhelmed. Nearly stupefied.

Plus, his inferred marriage proposal (via a letter to Mother only 12 days after we met), and his impulsive marriage declaration (at the Gramercy Inn Cocktail Lounge less than 24 hours after I'd served him), all complicated the whirlwind in my mind.

To achieve clarity, I weighed my options:

A. I could continue working on my feet every night, earning minimum wage plus tips, and worrying about my children during my evening shifts...or

B. I could take the offer from the man sitting outside in a Lincoln Continental, who said he'd pay me the same amount I was earning—in minimum wages and tips—to stay home and take care of my children.

He had kept every promise, followed through on every commitment, and was wonderful to my children. I had just met him and barely knew him but, you may wonder...did I take his offer to 'pay my wages and tips to stay home and care for my children' instead of going to work every night?

You're darned right I did. I then went to my supervisor at the Gramercy Inn Cocktail Lounge to turn in my re... no, not my resignation. I turned in a request for a six-month leave of absence. If something happened to Mr. Hamilton—like he suddenly died (or sobered up)—I'd need my old job back. I still had five children.

My manager was concerned about me. "Mary Anne, do you know what you're doing?"

My reply was, "I hope so."

———⬩———

Now that I didn't have to work every night, I had lots of time to get to know Mr. Hamilton, who asked that I call him *Laurens*, or *Laurie*. He was named after Alexander Hamilton's best friend, John Laurens.

My four-year-old son, John (*Lawrence* is his middle name), was only in preschool so he often came with me to the penthouse for lunch. The first time, Laurens asked the waiter to bring a pile of phone books to his dining room to prop up John's feet.

"There you go, Johnny," Laurens smiled. "Now your legs and feet don't have to dangle in the air so you'll be more comfortable." *Such thoughtfulness.* I began to see a different person than the egotistic narcissist I had initially perceived him to be.

Even though he still had not officially proposed to me, Laurens had a jeweler bring a tray of emerald and diamond rings to his suite. He wanted me to pick out a ring or design one, using the additional loose gems. He chose emeralds because the Hamilton Shield was green.

So, someone was paying me NOT to go to work, and then offered me an engagement ring, even though he had NOT officially proposed. Again, you may wonder, did I accept his gorgeous emerald and diamond ring?

You're darned right I did. I chose a beautiful emerald cut with six diamonds. After we were married, I discovered an appraisal showing my ring was worth $8,188 in 1965. I felt really bad that I'd worn it while painting the house and weeding the garden—without gloves.

For Christmas in 1965, Laurens took my five children, my friend and coworker Rosie, and me, on a private Pullman train car to the Omni Homestead Resort in Hot Springs, Virginia. Originally developed in 1766, it is the oldest resort in the nation. The Homestead has an elegant hotel with large adjacent luxury suites. We had a living room with a beautiful, decorated Christmas tree and a cozy fireplace. (More details on page 200.)

Laurens bought Rosie and me formal gowns in a hotel boutique. The kids liked skiing and skating with Rosie and I loved going horseback riding. We also enjoyed tea and treats in the hotel Grand Lobby during our five-day stay. It was an enchanting experience for our entire family.

On January 7, 1966, my oldest son, Leo, accompanied Laurens in a Navy plane to the Coast Guard Academy in New London, Connecticut. Laurens delivered the First Annual Alexander Hamilton Lecture, honoring his great-great-grandfather, and then stayed afterward to visit with the attendees. Leo didn't hear the speech, but he heard many positive comments about it from the cadets he met during their overnight stay.

As my 32nd birthday approached, Laurens had a furrier bring about 20 luxury stoles into his suite so I could pick out my birthday gift. Again, I was astonished by his generous extravagance, but I chose a beautiful white mink stole.

A week later, Laurens took me to New York along with my friend, Millie, (our chaperone). When we checked in to the Waldorf Astoria, North Tower, I could tell by the way he was greeted that Laurens had stayed there often.

We strolled along Fifth Avenue where Laurens bought me a beautiful black purse for $85. I had never paid that much for a purse. He took us to dinner at the Rainbow Room on the Rockefeller Center's 65th floor. Mesmerizing...the stunning view of Manhattan took our breath away. We listened to a great band during dinner and danced afterward. A horse-drawn carriage ride in Central Park completed our moon-lit evening.

On February 4, 1966, my 32nd birthday, Laurens hosted a party for me at a private dining room in the

Madison Hotel. He had purchased an airline ticket for my mother. He even booked a suite for Mother adjacent to his. Other family members attended, too. It was a wonderful party I will never forget.

I soon learned that Laurens occasionally served as a US government representative. He attended many events related to his great-great-grandfather.

President Eisenhower had designated Laurens as the chairman of the *Committee for the Birthplace and Boyhood Home of Alexander Hamilton*. On January 11, 1957, the 200th anniversary of Hamilton's birth, Laurens had affixed a plaque to the front wall of his great-great-grandfather's birthplace on Nevis in the West Indies.

Laurens attended the launch of the fifth USCGC *Hamilton* WPG-715 in New Orleans in mid-December, 1965, six weeks after we met. Although he was tending to official Coast Guard duties, he wrote numerous letters he hand delivered to me. He also brought me a beautiful jade necklace he'd picked out.

It had only been 60 days since I met Laurens, but they'd been filled with events, gifts, and memories. One day I was a struggling waitress and soon-to-be-divorced mother of five, needing friends and neighbors to help with childcare so I could work to pay the mortgage and provide for my children. A mere 30 days later, I was being paid to stay home to enjoy my children. No wonder I felt overwhelmed. Our lives seemed like a fantasy.

My gifts included a formal gown, an exquisite purse, a diamond and emerald ring, diamond earrings, two diamond and emerald brooches, a jade necklace, a mink stole, and I could have had a brand-new car. I found receipts later showing that the jewelry alone cost over $13,000, nearly what our College Park house cost in 1958. I'd also been escorted to fancy dinners, live shows, overnight train rides, luxury hotels, and elegant resorts.

I'd never asked for any of it...it just happened.
It seemed too good to be true...almost mythical.
But not only was it true, I soon discovered...
...that it was just the beginning.

CHAPTER 5
HISTORICAL DESTINATIONS

Speedboats, Yachts, Planes,
and the Queen

In early 1966, we were in New York City. Laurens wanted to show me the cemetery at Trinity Church, where the gravesites of Alexander Hamilton and other family members were located, but the gate was locked.

A man approached us. "This area is closed for construction. It's unsafe due to equipment and debris."

Laurens exploded. I was afraid he might strike the man with his cane.

"Alexander Hamilton was *my* great-great-grandfather," he bellowed. "We are going to enter *now* to pay our respects *now*."

We got in.

We also visited The Grange, the only home Alexander Hamilton had built for his family in 1801. What a sad sight. It had been wedged in between a church and an apartment building and was in disrepair. In 1924, Laurens' Uncle Jack (J. P. Morgan, Jr.) had purchased The Grange for the American Scenic and Historic Preservation Society. They had repaired it and filled it with period pieces, but after nearly 40 years, it was empty, locked, and closed to the public indefinitely. It desperately needed maintenance again. And a new location. *(See QR Code p. 199.)*

In 2008, The Grange was lifted 40 feet and then moved to its current location.

In 1962, Congress passed an act transferring The Grange's ownership to the National Park Foundation and the National Park Service. They renamed it The Hamilton Grange. The caretaker, Raleigh, still lived in the basement and greeted Laurens as if they had been long lost friends. He unlocked the door, gave us a tour, and asked us to sign the guestbook. I signed *Mary Anne Clark* because I was not yet a Hamilton.

The Morgan side of Laurens' family was also rich in national history. His mother, Juliet Pierpont Morgan, was the daughter of global financier John Pierpont (J. P.) Morgan and his wife, Frances. Laurens revealed his Morgan family stories as well as his Hamilton history.

The day after our moon-lit, horse-drawn carriage ride in New York, Laurens had the limo driver take us to the Metropolitan Club for lunch. Because some of his friends had been rejected by another club, J. P. Morgan had founded the exclusive Metropolitan Club in 1891 and was its first president. (More details about Laurens' grandfather are included on page 200.)

———◆———

Laurens was invited to represent the United States when Queen Elizabeth II and Prince Philip visited Nevis on February 22, 1966. What a thrill! He invited Chief, my brother, his wife, our mother, and me. We flew to Antigua in the Lesser Antilles on February 14, 1966.

Our chartered yacht was moored at Nelson's Dockyard in English Harbor.

The Sea Huntress was a 125-foot-long converted minesweeper. Also on board was an 18-foot inboard speedboat named the Playmate and an inflatable boat known as the Zodiac. The Sea Huntress was equipped with a hydraulic lift to lower and raise the swim platform and sea vessels when we wanted to swim or water-ski. Or go joyriding in the speedboat.

Captain Barry and his six crew members took great care of our party of six. They served us snacks and cocktails as well as catered meals, day and night.

L-R Standing: Ray (brother), Laurie; Seated: Ray's wife, Betsy, Mother, and me

Laurens had business dealings in St. John's, Antigua so the rest of us went along to go shopping.

The next day, we tried going to Guadeloupe, approximately 50 nautical miles to the south. Crashing waves off our deck forced us to return to English Harbor. It was calm but there was no dock space, so we had to anchor out. Captain Barry lowered the Playmate and my brother and I went water-skiing...well, he skied a lot, but I only got up once.

That evening, a floating contraption resembling a bath tub, rowboat, and canoe appeared out of the water's darkness with nine small boys ranging in age from 6 to 14. They came to the boarding platform and were playing calypso music on some of the most unusual instruments I've ever seen or heard: Coke bottles with the bottoms broken out covered with wax paper fastened by a rubber band, a two-string cello for a bass fiddle, a washboard and something resembling a trumpet. I invited them aboard and they played "All Day, All Night, Mary Anne." Despite their bizarre instruments, they sounded pretty good. We gave each of them a couple of dollars and their faces dazzled, as if we'd given them hundred-dollar bills.

On Thursday, February 17, the crew weighed anchor and we departed for Nevis, 60 nautical miles west of Antigua. An oval-shaped island, Nevis covers only 36 square miles. But Nevis Peak is 3,232 feet high and can be spotted from a great distance. It has a constant cloud over its peak.

We arrived at Nevis and my brother, his wife, and I walked along the beach. Two British West Indies boys about 11 or 12 years old joined us in the water. They only wore underwear and thought nothing of it. I asked them where the Catholic Church was. One boy said they'd be back the following Sunday to show us. They had a donkey so they jumped on his back and rode off.

On Sunday, Captain Barry and our French chef Eva picked up the boys, Floris and his brother, all dressed up in white shirts, ties, and khaki pants. Captain Barry took us all to shore in the Playmate and the boys walked a few blocks to attend Mass with Mother and me. (See page 206.)

After taking Mother and me to Mass, the boys visited the Sea Huntress. Captain Barry and Eva then took them back to shore.

Laurens had meetings with his lawyers regarding his divorce from wife #4, so he had to catch flights to and from other islands. After several missed charters, he finally returned, upset at the airlines, but happy to have his divorce completed. I was glad that my divorce had been finalized a few days before we left home.

We weighed anchor and returned to Nevis. Eva and I swam ashore and saw Alexander Hamilton's birthplace on the water's edge. A wall surrounded the property, which had a broken staircase in the courtyard. Shattered branches, weeds, and debris littered the grounds. The plaque that Laurens had unveiled for the Bicentennial of Alexander Hamilton's birth on January 11, 1957, was still attached to the outer wall. Later in the day, Laurens took me on my first tour of Nevis.

That evening, my brother had been asked to be one of five judges for the local beauty queen contest, so he and his wife and Captain Barry and Eva went ashore to a local tavern. Laurens had already gone to bed so I stayed in, too. (I really wanted to go, but Mother didn't think it was proper for me to go out without my fiancé.)

We later learned that the contestants and the venue were local, but the judges were visiting tourists so they could be impartial. The islands are so small that everyone knows everyone. Using tourists for judges was a win-win solution. The winner was a young lady named Miss Clark, no relation to me, as far as we knew. One advantage of staying in that night was I was well rested for our 'date' with the queen the following day.

We awoke to a distinct air of anticipation on Tuesday, February 22, 1966. Laurens was about to meet the world leaders representing the land from which our country received our independence nearly 200 years earlier.

It was also the 234th anniversary of the birth of our distinguished war general and first president, George Washington. Being an heir to Alexander Hamilton, General Washington's primary aide-de-camp, Laurens was perfect to represent the United States of America.

The harbor atmosphere was filled with energy in preparation for the royal pageantry. A huge red carpet stretched across the entire length of the dock and people were scurrying around. Small boats arrived and departed. We had a slight issue with the dock warden who would not let us tie up the Sea Huntress for water. But instead of challenging a nearby British destroyer, Captain Barry moved our yacht away from the dock and anchored out.

The dock steps were boarded up to accommodate the queen's visit. Her huge yacht was too large for the harbor so a smaller vessel was used for their transfer.

Dressed in a bright red uniform, the warden wielded a sword as he barked orders to his assistants. He sent word that we should bring Laurens in one of our boats to the dock via the beach since we could not use the boarded-up steps.

A beach transfer?! That was out of the question, especially in plain view of the dignitaries on the dock. He'd have had to wade ashore or be carried by an aide.

I put my foot down. "No!" I was indignant. "Laurens is representing the United States of America and should be treated with the dignity befitting his presence."

I repeatedly sent Captain Barry to convince the warden to dispatch a British Navy launch to our yacht.

After three tries, my demands were finally granted and the launch picked up Laurens. They took him to the dock, and then escorted him to his place in the receiving line.

Watching from the deck of the Sea Huntress, we saw the Britannia anchor. The queen and prince boarded a Navy launch to transport them to the dock. They descended the steps and began shaking hands with dozens of dignitaries in the receiving line. Wearing a bright yellow dress and hat, the queen and her entourage slowly moved down the line towards the waiting limousine motorcade.

Suddenly the queen stopped. We craned forward to see who she was speaking with. It was Laurens!

Queen Elizabeth II spoke with Laurens on a Nevis dock in 1966.

Royal protocol requires silence unless spoken to, so we knew the queen must have addressed Laurens first.

We were excited, wondering what had started their conversation, the longest chat they had with anyone.

Soon, everyone exited the dock in the motorcade and Laurens appeared on the shore. Alone.

Captain Barry and his first mate took the Zodiac to the beach to pick him up…literally. Barry lifted Laurens from the sand, hoisted him into the air, and seated him in the rubber boat. His tie was askew, but he appeared to be happy.

We were all anxious to hear about his conversation with the queen and the prince so we bombarded him with the same question. "What did they say?"

Laurens started to tease us. "They were very kind, and courteous…and diplomatic.…"

We became impatient. "Come on, Laurie, tell us. What did they ask? What did you say?"

"Well…" He finally relented, smiling. "Her Royal Highness appears to have studied history. She wanted to discuss the facts of how Alexander Hamilton personally assisted George Washington during the Revolutionary War and in the early process of creating our nation. She honored my great-great-grandfather's legacy more than most citizens in our own country."

At the time, I wasn't fully aware of Laurens' reasons for being so passionate about the importance of his family's legacy, but it seemed like he had gleaned some satisfaction after speaking with the queen and hearing her perceptions.

When our discussion ended, Captain Barry launched the Playmate so we could see the Britannia up close. As we circled the enormous yacht, we were met with cheers as the rails were lined with sailors, waving and whistling. Suddenly, I flew into the dashboard! A huge wave crashed into our boat at an odd angle and the impact threw me forward, cutting my lip open. For years, I referred to the mark on my lip as my 'queen scar.'

During the remainder of our time, we visited St. Croix, where we met intriguing people and saw interesting sights. After a taxi ride to the Buccaneer Hotel, we enjoyed the veranda overlooking the harbor. A St. Croix resident named Heidi joined us for dinner on the Sea Huntress. She was a hit with Laurens because they had mutual friends in New York, the yacht club, and Cape Cod. Laurens stayed up later than usual, chatting with her.

Heidi invited us to a local bar, and then later to her place for a night-cap. Laurens declined and went to bed early, as expected. But this time, I went out with the group, too. Heidi's home had a commanding view of the city and harbor. We could also see one of her neighbor's homes, owned by comedian-concert pianist, Victor Borge.

We departed St. Croix on March 1, 1966. In addition to having the experience of our lives—my seeing and Laurens' meeting Queen Elizabeth II and Prince Philip—we both now had our divorces finalized.

———◆———

Laurens' discussion with the queen motivated him to double his efforts to promote Alexander Hamilton's legacy in America. The man deserved honor... especially since a concerted effort to diminish his contributions had been ongoing for over one hundred sixty-two years. If the current leader of the opposing forces in the Revolutionary War honored Alexander Hamilton, shouldn't our nation's people—who benefited from the war's victory—acknowledge his contributions as well?

This Nevis trip gave me a glimpse of the world Laurens had to penetrate while trying to promote his great-great-grandfather's legacy. People wouldn't listen. If they did, most were not interested in pursuing the deeper truths beyond the basic Founding Father details.

That's why I've compiled three lists of facts highlighting my great-great-grandfather-in-law's accomplishments for this book. I've inserted these features, called *Laurens' Lists A, B, and C,* into this memoir.

As mentioned, I believe these little-known truths are as valuable as the true stories about my life, if not more so.

My hope is that all readers will be inspired to learn more about the many actions and deeds Alexander Hamilton contributed to the creation of the greatest nation on earth, our United States of America.

Many, if not all, of the documented facts resulted from research by my good friend Michael E. Newton considered one of, if not *the* premier of all the Hamilton scholars and history experts. He made exhaustive efforts to delve into exclusive archives, domestic and abroad. He hired interpreters, translators, and scholars to help decode primary documents, many written in foreign languages. I am extremely grateful for Michael's work and his willingness to share his research and documentation.

My friend Michael E. Newton and I enjoyed a relaxing moment in New York City in July, 2018.

Laurens' Lists of Hamilton Facts

ounding Father Alexander Hamilton overcame extreme obstacles and made tremendous contributions towards creating our nation. Because I was busy raising five children—and working—during our 12 years of marriage, I didn't fully appreciate my husband, Laurens' frustrations when his great-great-grandfather did not receive the national honor and respect he deserved. After experiencing *Hamilton, An American Musical* in 2016, my eyes were opened. Gradually, I learned many facts that had been suppressed for centuries. Most truths are still relatively unknown, and new discoveries are still being made.

I'm posting three Laurens' Lists, so named because my late husband was passionate about these facts, even though some were not documented until after he passed away. List A focuses on Hamilton's childhood and teen years. List B highlights his education and military service. List C details his family and his contributions towards the creation, foundation, and maturation of our great nation.

Laurens' List "A"
Unique Childhood Circumstances Hamilton Overcame

1. Reportedly, he was born on the West Indies island of Nevis on January 11, 1757 (or 1755). Recent documentation supports the 1755 year of birth, but other records show he may have been born in 1754.

2. His mother, Rachel Faucett Lavien, who descended from the French Huguenots, taught him to read and write in French. Eventually, he was able to read and translate Greek and Latin (for his schooling), and he was probably familiar with Dutch from his childhood on St. Eustatius as well as Danish from his years on St. Croix.

3. His father, James Hamilton, was thought to be the fourth son of a Scottish Laird, who moved from Scotland to the West Indies seeking his fortune.

4. Due to his mother's divorce restrictions, his parents couldn't marry; thus, he and his brother were illegitimate children.

5. Barred from certain schools due to his birth status, he attended private schools.

6. He was primarily self taught; his mother had many books and he was a voracious reader.

7. At a young age, he handled accounts and merchandizing for his mother's small store.

8. About age nine, after his father left and never returned, he began writing essays and poetry.

9. About age 10, he began working at a local merchant's import/export business as a store clerk and general assistant.

10. At age 12, he and his mother were very sick. After she died, his uncle became his guardian, but he died, too.

11. He reportedly lived with various families and friends, and, possibly with his employer, Nicholas Cruger.

12. As a young teenager, he continued working at the import-export business. For five months during Mr. Cruger's absence, he handled all business transactions, including entire ship cargoes and decisions about voyages.

13. Many island business leaders recognized his skills and talents and raised funds for him.

14. His mentor, Rev. Hugh Knox, and others, suggested he go to New York to get his education.

15. In August, 1772, a devastating hurricane struck the islands, leveling nearly everything.

16. He wrote a stirring description of the hurricane that was published in the *Royal Danish American Gazette*.

17. Employers and businessmen wrote letters for him; others contributed funds towards his education.

18. He set sail towards New York in the fall of 1772.

19. Reportedly, his ship caught fire. It was extinguished, possibly, by the crew and passengers using buckets of sea water.

20. He finally docked in Boston and had to find transportation to New York City.

21. He eventually arrived in New York in October or November, 1772.

22. He contacted referred associates, who helped with housing, food, and clothing.

23. Island business contacts had set up funding sources for his initial living expenses.

CHAPTER 6
REMARRIAGE DESTINY

*Georgetown Pike Estate and
Prince George Wedding*

B e careful what you wish for.

When Leo and I were evicted for having too many children in a 2-bedroom apartment, I wondered what it might be like to have a huge home where we could have all five children and no one could make us leave. I was about to find out.

Laurens was excited. "Let's go for a ride. I want to show you something." It was early March, 1966, and we had just returned from our visit with the queen in tropical Nevis. Chief was at the wheel of the Lincoln.

We drove down Old Georgetown Pike towards Great Falls, Virginia, and turned onto a dirt road. After about a half mile, we saw a tennis court on the right and a two-car garage with a one-bedroom apartment on top. On the far side was a delightful swimming pool, with two dolphins spewing water from their mouths into the pool. Swaying trees provided a peaceful wooded backdrop behind the pool. The driveway circled around the front of a beautiful manor. The side yard looked down onto the Potomac River. Laurens had found a gorgeous estate in a serene setting. He'd already leased it and was moving in.

At the Lindwood Estate, our family enjoyed swimming, tennis, and a view of the Potomac.

Chief parked in the circular driveway and we alighted from the Lincoln. I was excited as Laurens unlocked the door and we stepped inside.

"What an entry," I exclaimed. It led to the middle of a huge hallway. "It must be 40 feet long and 8 feet wide… and look at the high ceilings and the two huge windows!"

The majestic living room with a fireplace and high double doors was to the right. On either side of the fireplace, two sets of high glass doors opened onto the stately side patio overlooking the Potomac River. The elegant dining room adjoined the living room.

On the left, down the long, front entrance hallway, was a cozy den with another fireplace and double glass doors, leading to a screened porch. The gourmet kitchen was in the back.

"Wow!" I gushed. As I marveled, Laurens beamed.

A spacious master suite with a full bath was on the main floor. The suite also had a screened porch. Another bedroom and bath were adjacent. *This is John's room* I thought. *He's only four, so I want him near me.*

I was breathless, but there was more. The staircase near the kitchen led to the second floor with a bath and multiple bedrooms, all with dormer windows overlooking the woods or the river. This Lindwood Estate was a far cry from our tiny 2-bedroom apartment, where we'd been evicted after four of our five children had been born.

———•———

As far as I can recall, Laurens never officially proposed marriage to me, unless you count a poem he wrote in the middle of a blizzard as a proposal. I'd been born during a DC blizzard so it seemed almost fitting that I received a poetic *potential* proposal, written in the midst of a DC blizzard in late January, 1966.

Lines From a Suitor to His Fair Lady

Oh, you are there and I am here because of winter weather

You know I'm never happy, dear, when we can't be together

So be my wife and share my life; we shall be seldom parted

If you say "no," I'll have to go through my life broken-hearted

I'm sure that we are meant to be, both fast and friendly mated

So you can always be with me, when I go where I'm fated

LMH 1-30-66

Back then, it seemed as if he'd told so many people that he was going to marry me, he might have *felt* like he'd already asked. There was an unspoken expectation but I still was not sure if we should proceed.

After seeing his poem and reading parts of his speech he gave at the Coast Guard Academy in January, 1966, I began to see Laurie in a different light. When he talked about the christening of USCGC *Hamilton* WHEC-715 in New Orleans back in December, he appeared to be fun-loving and witty and charming. It was refreshing because he seemed so down-to-earth,…not stuffy and proper all the time. Here's the part of Laurie's speech that revealed an endearing part of him to me:

> "As many of you may know, on the Mississippi they have to launch them (Coast Guard cutters) thwartwise. It isn't wide enough to let them go stern-first, so you see this vessel up on a levee, and a lady smacks it with champagne and something happens and the next thing you know, the whole darn thing is slipping to leeward and it lands in there with an awful splash, shakes itself a couple of times like a terrier…and then floats proudly." (See QR Code p. 199.)

When I first read it, it sounded like he was having fun. It made me realize there was more to his personality than I had originally perceived. We'd only met eight weeks before his speech, but that's when I decided to give our relationship a chance.

For the next several weeks, we enjoyed each other's company, relaxing, traveling, and getting to know each other. He was extremely kind to the children and he was never pushy or aggressive. I began to see how our relationship might actually work.

In March, 1966, it had been four months since I left the Gramercy Inn Cocktail Lounge. Mild panic began to set in. *My six months' leave of absence is almost over so maybe we'd better set a date.*

On our next outing, I casually mentioned, "I've been thinking…I like full moons. I was born on February 4th and May 4th will be a full moon, too. How about having our wedding on Wednesday, May 4th, at the Prince George Court House Justice of the Peace chambers?"

"That sounds fine with me." He was so agreeable.

I had a gorgeous ring, Laurens had found an estate, and we now had a date. *Who needs an official proposal?*

I was Laurens' fifth wife so we had a small family affair with a luncheon at the Hilton after the wedding.

After our May 4, 1966 wedding, we posed for a photo at home with our poodle, Bruno.

When the children's school year ended in June, we all moved in with Laurens at the Lindwood Estate and I rented my College Park house to a nice couple. Laurens had hired an older pair to cook and take care of the house. They'd lived above the garage in the one-bedroom apartment until questions about their integrity indicated it was not going to work out. They were let go.

Laurens' nurse, Mrs. Burns, took over meal prep and housekeeping. She was the nicest person whom we all loved and affectionately called "Mrs. B." She and her husband had raised four children, so she knew how to take care of a household. She even made the kids clean their pets' litter boxes. Chief picked her up in the morning. She prepared and cleaned up after breakfast and lunch and then cooked dinner before leaving at 4 p.m.

We had a groundskeeper, Lindberg, who maintained the swimming pool and the expansive grounds. In the winter, he cleaned the fireplaces out in the morning and reset them. We also had a cleaning woman who came in twice a week.

Like I said, be careful what you wish for. I know this all sounds great, but if you're like me and you weren't raised having servants, it's hard to sit and not want to get up and help clean the windows and do the other household chores. I often felt guilty and didn't want to seem lazy by reading the paper while the hired helpers were working. I tried to relax, but it never felt comfortable.

Laurens wrote to the Admiral Farragut Academy in St. Petersburg, Florida, near where Mother lived, and enrolled the two oldest boys. I was happy that Leo and Mike would be in a great school and get an excellent education. Kitty and Anna would go to the nearby public school and John would start kindergarten at a private school down the street.

"Laurie, I'd like to go to school, too," I announced one day. "You own a radio station so I want to go to broadcast school to get a broadcasting license."

"That's fine with me," he replied. Laurens owned Radio Station WEER in Warrenton, Virginia. At broadcast school, I was popular. In addition to being the only woman in my classes, I also had a husband who owned an entire radio station.

———◆———

In May, 1967, the brand-new USCGC *Hamilton* - WHEC-715 came to Washington's Navy yard and was open for public inspection. The staff was exceptionally accommodating when I called to inform them I was coming to see the new cutter.

"Mrs. Hamilton, can we come to get you and drive you down?"

"Thanks," I replied. "My daughter, Anna, is coming with me so I'll drive us."

When we arrived, the entire crew was standing in what appeared to be an official line in honor of us at the top of the gangplank.

"What is this?" I whispered subtly to Anna. I was 33 years old and it was my first time experiencing something like this. Anna was more poised than me... and she was barely ten.

The Cutter Hamilton 715 officers showed Anna and me a framed copy of the music for *The Cutter Hamilton Quick Step,* which the band had played for us.

"I think we're supposed to walk up through the middle of them," Anna replied, taking my arm.

We felt very special. I discovered later that this respectful reception created an experience referred to as being 'piped aboard,' initially named for the pipe that was played to honor dignitaries. If we had served in the military, they all would have been saluting us as we proceeded up the gangplank.

"Right this way," the officer directed us. "This is a brand-new, state-of-the-art 378-foot cutter that is powered by diesel and aircraft type jet engines. It's equipped with closed-circuit TV, providing surveillance of all important shipboard areas from the bridge." They showed us every part of the ship. The brand-new cutter *Hamilton 715* was modern, sparkling clean, and extremely impressive.

Living at the Lindwood Estate was a wonderful experience. Not only was it beautiful, spacious, and peaceful, but it was also involved in a dramatic piece of history that was featured in a *Reader's Digest 'Drama in Real Life'* story in the 1960s.

One winter day as I returned home, I noticed a jeep parked in the circular driveway. Inside our front door were large pools of water on the entryway floor. *What in the world?* Smaller puddles led to the den where a roaring fire was as bright as it was hot. Blankets were strewn on the floor and a hot water bottle was on the mantel beside a half-empty brandy snifter.

I was bewildered. "What's going on?" Laurens, Chief, Lindberg, and Mrs. B. all looked as if they were in shock.

Laurens described the scene I had missed. "If you had been here 15 minutes ago, you would have seen two people lying in front of the fireplace, wrapped in blankets, and shaking uncontrollably. The rescue squad was here. They and the ambulances just left."

Mrs. B. was gathering and folding the blankets, shaking her head in wonder. "They fell into the river and nearly didn't make it out."

"Who fell into the river?" I queried. This seemed unbelievable. *Why would anyone be out on the river when it was nearly frozen?*

Laurens began to explain. "I saw the jeep come up the hill from the river on that old path. I'm glad we were all here to meet them, a man and a woman. Their soaked clothes and hair were nearly frozen stiff and the lady was turning blue when Chief and Lindberg carried her in."

He turned to Lindberg. "Thanks for making such a roaring fire. And thank you, Mrs. B., for getting the blankets, hot water bottle and for pouring some brandy."

"They were mostly incoherent but said something about a rowboat and new camera lens," Laurens mused. "Maybe we'll find out more when they come to get the jeep."

The next day, I answered the knock at the front door. "Good morning, may I help you?"

"Hello…" the man looked puzzled. "Uhhhh…I was here with my wife yesterday and…" Laurens came around the corner and the man's face brightened with recognition.

"Oh, there he is…hello, sir." He shook Laurens' hand and came in as I shut the door.

"This is my wife, Mary Anne, and my name is Laurens. So glad to see you again."

He took off his hat. "My wife and I can't thank you enough for being here and helping us yesterday."

"You're very welcome. Come in and sit down. Can we get you a cup of coffee? Brandy?"

He smiled but remained standing. "No, thank you. I need to get back to the hospital."

Laurens grew solemn. "How's your wife doing?"

He rubbed his chin. "Much better today, thanks to you folks. The doctors said that 88 degrees is the lowest temperature a person can have and fully recover. Her body temperature was 92 degrees two hours after we got out of the freezing river. Hopefully, she'll recover."

Without thinking, I blurted, "What were you doing on the river and how'd you fall in?"

Laurens gently touched my arm but it was too late. "He needs to go, dear."

"No, no, it's fine." The man was patient. "We live just down the ridge. I have a new camera lens and it was sunny, so we rowed out to get pictures of our house and the river with all the snow. But we hit a rock and our boat capsized. It was so cold, we barely had enough strength to reach the bank and crawl to our jeep." He put his hat back on and reached out his hand. "I do need to get going now. Thank you again."

Laurens shook his hand while I opened the door and smiled at him as he departed. I later discovered that his personal account of their ordeal entitled "Death and the Friendly River," was published in the January, 1968 edition of *Reader's Digest. (See QR Code p. 208.)*

As the saying goes, all's well that ends well. For the nearly frozen couple, it appeared they would have a happy ending.

For our family, however, happy days were potentially on the verge of coming to an end.

CHAPTER 7
DESTINATION: DESTITUTION

Baldonia, Fund Woes,
Waitressing, Moving

Alittle history puts the following into perspective.

When Laurens' maternal grandfather, John Pierpont (J. P.) Morgan, died in 1913, he left his three daughters and his sons-in-law millions of dollars, and his only son, J. P. Morgan, Jr. received the rest of his estate, valued at over 2 billion dollars in today's markets. His mother, Juliet Pierpont Morgan

Hamilton passed away in 1952, so Laurens inherited his share. By then he had married four times and had no children, but he had great friends.

Laurens' best friend for several decades was Russell Arundel, founder and CEO of Pepsi Cola Long Island, a newspaperman, author, lobbyist, fox hound master, and avid outdoorsman. At first, he seemed to be a subdued and reserved guy, but I'll never forget his question to me back when Laurens first introduced us.

"Mary Anne, did Laurie tell you about the new nation we created near Canada?"

"No, I didn't, Prince, you tell her." Laurie always called Russell 'Prince' and this story revealed the reason.

Russell spoke quietly but with an air of pride. "I love the outdoors, especially fishing. Back in the '40s, I discovered an island just off Nova Scotia during a tuna fishing contest. I claimed it and bought it for $750 and renamed it 'The Principality of Outer Baldonia.' And I appointed myself the 'Prince of Princes.' " He patted his chest proudly.

I furrowed my brows, unsure if he was making up a story. But Laurie was smiling so I went along.

Russell didn't break stride. "When my buddies passed a fishing test, I designated them as royalty.

We wrote up a Declaration of Independence, which read, in part: *Fishermen are endowed with unalienable rights: the right to lie and be believed; the right of freedom from questioning, nagging,*

shaving, interruption, women, taxes, politics, war...
and the right to swear, lie, drink, gamble, and
be silent..."

He took a breath. "There's more, but you get the gist. We then created currency, coins, passports, our own military, and my daughter designed our national flag!"

My eyes widened. "Are you serious?"

Laurie was chuckling so I still wasn't sure if I could believe either of them.

"Yes," Russell continued, unfazed by my disbelief. "Women were banned from the island, for their own protection, but we made exceptions for membership. My secretary did all the paperwork and my daughter was our royal historian. But they never visited. No one could guarantee what they might see because members were allowed to let down all guard, clothing included."

Laurie began laughing and Russell became more animated. "You should have seen the response we got when I listed Outer Baldonia in the Washington, DC phone directory."

"You did what?" This was too bizarre. I shook my head, refusing to be suckered in.

Russell stopped. "She doesn't believe me, does she. Go get the coin, Laurie."

Laurie left the room and Russell continued calmly, trying to be serious. "This was the same time that the United Nations was processing multiple requests for memberships. They found my DC phone directory listing and invited Outer Baldonia to a United Nations meeting." I shook my head in disbelief.

Laurie returned and handed me a dime-sized coin that bore a circular label "Principality of Outer Baldonia" embossed around the edge. Russell's profile and the year 1948 were imprinted on the reverse side. My disbelief turned to pure astonishment. It *was* true.

Russell was reinvigorated. "When the Russians discovered our charter papers, their official state publication called me a 'tyrant whose aim was to make savages of my subjects by giving them the right to ignore ethical and moral laws established by mankind.' "

I shared his outrage. "They actually printed that?"

"Yes, they did. So...our little Principality of Outer Baldonia declared war on Russia on March 9, 1953!" Russell and Laurie roared with laughter. "They thought I had 'subjects'...but all we had was a herd...a herd of hapless sheep on a 4 acre rock!"

I joined in their laughter so it was difficult to talk. "What...what happened to avoid war?"

Russell finally got control. "The US and Canada ridiculed the Russians for reacting to our spoof in a derogatory Soviet state publication article. I wrote them a letter, demanding an apology, or we would sever our national ties. No one ever wrote back...so that's how I won the war against Russia." He pumped his fist as we all continued basking in our laughter.

I didn't realize until much later what a privilege it was to hear that great story first hand, before it evolved into a legendary tale shared by local tour guides—as well as on the internet—in the years to come.

As time went by, I also discovered that Russell was more passionate about preserving the great outdoors than he was towards nation-building. He eventually sold Baldonia for $1 to the Nova Scotia Bird Society on the condition that they name it after his brother. It was the *Earle E. Arundel Breeding Bird Sanctuary* for many decades. What an impacting first impression Russell made on me. Laurie loved him like a brother for over 30 years. *(See QR Code p. 208.)*

SALAMAR ~ SA was for Laurens' wife, the LA was for Laurens, MA was for Russell's wife, and the R was for Russell.

Laurie and Russell were such good friends that they bought an 85-foot yacht together named the SALAMAR. After outfitting it with the finest of everything, they hired the captain and crew on board, and moored it in Miami, Florida, and Washington, DC. Their favorite motoring waters were the Atlantic, the Caribbean, and the Gulf of Mexico.

They also bought a camp near the presidential retreat, Camp David, in Maryland. Later, Russell gave the yacht to Laurie, who signed the camp over to Russell. The yacht was sold before I met Laurie, but I still have dishes embossed with the New York Yacht Club burgee and Laurens' blue and yellow burgee, mementos of their fun-loving capers.

Unfortunately, things began to unravel and soon, all that remained were memories.

———◆———

In addition to buying luxuries and experiencing life to the fullest, Laurens was very generous with his funds. He'd waived military pay. Honorariums he was offered were donated back. He loved me and the children and gave me an allowance to take the kids out to have fun doing anything we wanted to do. His lavish lifestyle and giving heart were a risky combination. And because *professional philanthropists* have no pension or social security benefits, he was in a perilous position.

Laurens seldom consulted his financial experts, and when he did, he rarely followed their advice. In 1967, his accountant informed him that he owed the IRS big time. Stocks attached to his fourth divorce had sold and triggered a staggering capital gains tax liability. In current values, it was over a half million dollars. Money he no longer had. He'd have to liquidate assets to cover it.

Depreciating stocks and bond values, four divorces, and alimony payments had steadily depleted Laurens' portfolio. His generosity and carefree lifestyle had finally caught up with him.

Laurens' life had taken quite a turn and the transition hit him hard. He'd thought he had unlimited resources all of his life. Now he had to sell his prized radio station to cover his taxes. His health was failing but he couldn't afford to pay his private nurse.

We had lived at Lindwood for a year and Laurens had renewed the lease for another year. At first, I don't think he knew I was aware that his bank accounts were steadily dwindling. I told the property owner that we needed to break the lease. He had wanted to sell the property anyway, so I started looking for a house to buy in McLean, Virginia. That's when Laurens discovered I knew about our financial status.

Laurens became despondent. Because of his diminishing bank funds and health issues, he didn't want to go out or see any of his friends. We let Chief go because Laurens no longer went anywhere. I picked up John from school, and Mrs. B. drove herself. She realized our financial hardship and eventually offered to retire.

A wonderful McLean, Virginia home was vacant on Mori Street. It had plenty of room and was in a great location. In fact, it was just a couple miles from one of Jackie Bouvier Kennedy's childhood family homes.

We left Lindwood and moved to the Mori Street house on October 31, 1967, Halloween. Coincidently, I found a female black cat in the backyard tree and named her 'Spooky.' She lived to be about 20 years old.

———————◆———————

Russell helped us sell the radio station so we had some income from the mortgage Laurens took back. In 1969, I returned to waitressing, working dinner hours at a Steak House restaurant to help pay some bills. Laurens was home with the children, who affectionately called him "Skipper." They got to know him better because he stayed home *all* the time.

My daughter, Kitty, recalled a specific time that Skipper needed something typed up, but he no longer had a secretary. Because Kitty knew shorthand, he dictated to her and she typed it for him. He made her feel really special with his appreciation for the great job she had done.

In addition to taking my oldest son, Leo, to the Coast Guard Academy, Laurens helped him apply to the Admiral Farragut Academy in Florida. Leo stayed all four years. Mother paid for Leo's final year's tuition.

My second son, Michael's year at Farragut was difficult. He had to march off demerits on Saturdays. He resented having to take orders from someone who was shorter than his shoulders. He also didn't like having to cut his hair. After a year, he moved back home.

One night while I was at work, John had a traumatic encounter and he helped save Skipper's life.

Laurens was a chain smoker who was careless with his cigarettes. In early March, 1971, after he'd had his sleeping pill and scotches, Laurens fell asleep in the recliner and dropped a lit cigarette on his lap.

John, who was only nine years old, had walked into the living room, saw Laurens' gown smoldering, and yelled for help. "Skipper's gown is smoking! Call the fire department!" John's older siblings heard his cry and called the firemen.

The kids called me at work and I hurried to the hospital, which was owned by a very good doctor. He and Laurens had been personal friends for many years.

Laurens was in the burn unit for three months with severe injuries on both thighs, his stomach, and his chest. Most of the time he was in an induced coma but I still visited him nearly every day.

When he was released from the hospital, he became even more depressed and withdrawn. Cigarettes and scotch were both off limits. He stayed in his room, watched TV, and worked on crossword puzzles.

I was so grateful that Mrs. B. had him sign up for Medicare when the program began in 1965, the same year Laurens turned 65. At least some of his medical bills were covered.

One afternoon on my way to work, I stopped in Georgetown to visit Laurens' sister, Helen Hamilton Burgess, widow of Undersecretary of the Treasury, W. Randolph Burgess. I was wearing my waitress uniform, so I think she then understood that I would always work in order to care for her brother. A few years later, she started sending us money every month, and she even continued for a year after Laurens passed away. God bless her. It had never occurred to me to ask for money.

While working at the Steak House restaurant, I got to know one of my customers, a man named Stanley who worked nearby. Our friendship lasted for the next 28 years. I thought of him as my best friend.

———◆———

In the fall of 1971, my brother and his wife moved to St. Petersburg, Florida to be nearer to Mother.

I had resigned from the Steak House and we had a small income from the radio station. I thought *Why am I staying in Virginia?* I told Laurens we were moving to Florida.

"Florida?" he protested. "It's so flat there."

"You never leave the house anyway. Sign here." He signed the documents, putting our McLean, Virginia house on the market. I sold my home in College Park, Maryland to the tenants, and then I flew to St. Petersburg to buy a house.

My brother had already been looking for houses for us. When I arrived, he had picked out a few to preview. Pinellas Point was a beautiful location, near my brother's home and not too far from Mother's.

When we looked at the second house, I had one thought: *Perfect*. There was just one problem. Our McLean, Virginia home sale had not yet closed so we didn't have the down payment.

I knew Laurens would not be happy, but I called Russell for help, telling him we'd pay him back when our Virginia home sale closed.

Russell was beside himself. "All the money's gone, Mary Anne? All of it?" He then realized why he hadn't seen Laurie since he'd helped us sell the radio station.

We wrote a contract and set the closing for Christmas time, 1972, when the children were out of school. By then Leo Jr. was married to Brenda, a girl he had met while at Farragut. They were already living near Mother. Kitty and Michael wanted to stay in the DC area, so they took Spooky, our cat, and moved in with their father. Anna and John moved to Florida with us.

Laurens and the children stayed at Mother's place while my friend, Stanley, helped me drive our family car from Virginia to Florida. We also had our family dog, a vintage original painting of Laurens' mother, and an exclusive original portrait of Alexander Hamilton, as well as numerous Hamilton and Morgan family mementos.

I finished the closing procedure on our Virginia house and repaid Russell his down payment. After we got settled in our new home, I began looking for work.

The Crown Liquor, an upscale cocktail lounge in St. Petersburg, was where I landed a bartending job. One of my responsibilities was counting the till at the end of my shift. Occasionally, the till funds were short so I added a few coins or bills from the tips in my pocket to reconcile it. Never more than three dollars.

For some reason, this bar made employees take random lie-detector tests. One question on my test was, "Did you do anything to alter the amount of money you counted at night?"

I lied and said "no." I had never taken money, only added it out of my pocket when necessary.

I flunked the test.

They wanted to give me a two-week suspension and I assumed they would then fire me.

So I quit.

They lost one of the best employees they ever had, a hard-working, non-drinking, honest bartender.

I didn't know it then, but by quitting and voluntarily *losing* that job, I *actually gained* an opportunity to launch my dream career of a lifetime.

CHAPTER 8
PREDESTINED HEALTH DECLINE

Career, Caregiver,
Sea Ceremony, Trips

A few years later in 1976, my friend, Stanley, moved from Maryland to St. Petersburg. He worked as a comptroller and also did taxes. When he enrolled at St. Petersburg Jr. College to take their real estate courses, I decided to tag along and get my credentials, too. After completing the course, we aced the exams and earned our real estate licenses.

After merely accompanying a friend to real estate classes, I inadvertently discovered what eventually became my destiny career. It was a good thing that back in 1976, it didn't require a college degree or even a high school diploma. I had neither.

I started working for a company near Mother's home in northeast St. Petersburg. It paid well and its potential could be determined by my willingness to work hard. Plus, I took to it like a duck to water. In fact, I have a trunk full of top listing and selling awards I earned during my career, spanning over 38 years. I closed my last real estate deal in 2014, when I was 80 years old.

Of all the well-paying careers I could have pursued, real estate was the best for us.

Why?

Scheduling. With few exceptions, I could schedule appointments around Laurens' care needs. His health was declining rapidly. He needed more assistance as I began my new career.

It had been a difficult transition from being an independently wealthy, nationally known patriot, to losing both his wealth and health simultaneously. In spite of our challenges, Laurens had been wonderful to my five children and me during one of the most difficult times of my life. I was determined to be here for him until he no longer needed me. My resume included *full-time caregiver* along with *novice real estate agent* for the next few years.

Laurens passed away peacefully in his sleep on February 8, 1978, just five months shy of his 78th birthday. I was with him until the very end, determined that he receive the honor and dignity he deserved for his final days, his closing ceremony, and his ultimate resting place.

At the funeral home, I asked the director to call Admiral Owen Siler, Commandant, US Coast Guard, who had been with Laurens on the trip to Nevis for the 1957 Hamilton Bicentennial. They'd been old friends and the Admiral called right back. I informed him of Laurens' passing, and he asked if there was anything he could do. I told him Laurens had always wanted to have his ashes taken out to sea on the *Hamilton* 715 (The official title was USCGC *Hamilton* WHEC-715 but Laurens shortened it.) He hoped his remains would float back to Nevis and St. Croix, where Hamilton had lived.

The Admiral told me the *Hamilton* 715 was in Norfolk, Virginia and would be at the US Naval Base, Mayport, in Jacksonville, Florida, in the middle of March. I was happy that my family and I could meet the cutter Laurens requested here in Florida.

Captain Flanders would be in immediate charge of the ceremony. When the ship got to the Gulf Stream and Sargasso Sea, Laurens' ashes were to be consigned to the deep. I was very impressed with the concern being shown within the top Coast Guard circles in Washington, DC. They assured me that everything was being done to make the ceremony something very special. The details were carefully worked out and it was to be covered by the press reporters and photographers.

On March 16, I met Captain Flanders who informed me that the ceremony would be performed by the ship's company on Saturday morning, March 18, 1978, off the East Coast, perhaps in the vicinity of the Gulf Stream. Captain Flanders told me they would love to be able to take me along to experience the ceremony at sea, but they were heading for Guantanamo Bay and they didn't have a way to bring me back. I stayed in Florida.

The Coast Guard provided a descriptive accounting of the ceremony:

> On Saturday morning at 0800, the ship's company was present in full dress muster and the vessel stopped. The flag was at half-mast. The sun brightened the gold and blue uniforms surrounding the urn and the folded flag in front of the chaplain as he repeated the scripture and prayers. He honored Laurens' service to our country, his association with the Coast Guard, and the commissioning ceremony of this ship (which had occurred exactly eleven years ago, on March 18, 1967). He repeated words Laurens spoke in his first annual Alexander Hamilton lecture at the Coast Guard Academy, where he called Coast Guardsmen "Patriots," admonishing them to thoroughly train themselves. He also mentioned the scriptures from the last paragraph of Laurens' lecture: II Timothy 4:7: I have fought a good fight, I have finished my course, I have kept the faith.

An escort of six ensigns carried the flag and then distributed the ashes. A guard fired three rifle volleys, and a sonar technician played taps.

According to the report, it was a beautiful sea ceremony and life celebration for a wonderful patriot. He had tried his hardest to fulfill his mission, helping America complete its course, making our world a better place, and promoting his great-great-grandfather's legacy.

Only six days before Laurens passed, his best friend, Russell, died on Thursday, February 2, 1978. He was 75. During Laurens' last days, he recorded his condolences on tape to Russell's wife, Marjorie. I was going to type it but I sent her the tape so she could hear Laurens' voice.

Two days after Laurens passed away, Russell's son, Nick, wrote me a beautiful letter, thanking me for my devotion to Laurie. It read in part:

February 10, 1978

Dear Mary Anne,

*   ...You have been one of the most extraordinary, loving, and warm human beings I have ever known. I only hope the years you gave to Laurie have been as rewarding to you as the immense regard in which you are held by all of us who came to know you through him....*

*   Affectionately, Nick*

As I've mentioned often, the years I spent with Laurens were extremely rewarding for me, as well. I'm grateful to his best friend, Russell and his son, Nick, and all of Laurie's friends and acquaintances who enriched my life over the years.

———◆———

After caring for Laurens for such a long time, I missed him, but refocused my sights on my real estate career. In addition to earning our real estate agent licenses, Stanley and I had also passed the real estate broker's exam. Although he opted not to change careers, he was very supportive of mine. Our friendship continued until he died in 1995 after a prolonged illness.

In February, 1979, I put my house on the market, sold it quickly, and bought a condominium in Seminole, Florida, where I still reside. With some of the funds from selling my home, I purchased a house in North St. Petersburg and rented it to my daughter, Anna.

Real estate gave me an opportunity to help many people, and I was very good at my career. But if anyone had told me to go to classes to learn to be an agent, my thoughts would have been *I could never do that. I didn't even finish high school.*

I'm glad I challenged myself to stretch beyond my own self-imposed limits. That's a lesson we can all benefit from in every aspect of life.

Because I had my broker's license, I considered opening my own real estate brokerage. One of my favorite songs I sang as a 1940s teenager was "Over the Rainbow." I had applied for "Rainbow" as a vanity license plate in 1980, but someone already had it. Thus, I accepted my second choice "Rainboe" and it's still mounted on my 1999 Cadillac DeVille today. (See photo on page 207.)

As it turned out, it would have been a mistake for me to own my own real estate brokerage named "Rainbow Realty." It was good that someone beat me to that name by a week. I was much better suited to be an agent rather than an administrator. Years later, when the rainbow became a recognizable symbol, people who saw my license often asked, "Are you gay or gay friendly?" I love all people so I always answer the latter.

———◆———

In addition to building my career, I began taking trips to various local, regional, national, and international destinations.

Mother and I drove to Washington, DC to visit family in the spring of 1981. While we were there, my best friend from high school, Jackie Ignacio, invited me to have lunch on June 4th. Our birthdays were 3 days apart so at age 47, we had been friends for over 30 years.

Jackie had worked on Capitol Hill since high school. Over the years, she assisted many lawmakers, including Senator Connie Mack.

On June 3rd, she called me to change our lunch time. "Come later so you can see Mother Teresa."

"How?" She was a wonderful servant of God and I never dreamed I'd get to see her in person.

Jackie explained. "She's being presented an award by a US agency and I reserved two seats, but we have to be discreet."

"Why?" I was always up for an adventure and started to giggle.

Jackie was serious. "Just trust me, I'll see you at 1:30 at…" she named a secret location.

The next day, Jackie had a huge ring of jangling keys. "Ta Dah! C'mon." She grabbed my hand and we headed down a narrow hallway. Locked doors, key jingles, another dark hallway. It kind of felt like we were sneaking around in the bowels of the Capitol…because we were.

The final door was the room where the presentation was being held. Jackie's two seats in the front row were still open. A Distinguished Public Service Award was presented to Mother Teresa by the US Secretary of Health and Human Services. It was a privilege to witness.

Afterward, a staffer asked us, "Do you want to meet Mother Teresa?"

We jumped up and I handed my camera to Jackie. After introductions and greetings, Jackie took my picture and then I took hers. What a great honor.

My friend, Jackie, and I met Mother Teresa in 1981 when she received an award.

When I showed my picture of Mother Teresa and me to a coworker at the office where I worked, she quipped, "The saint and the sinner." We shared a good laugh.

My Journal: In 1983, The Right Excellent and Right Honourable, Dr. Sir Kennedy A. Simmonds, the first Prime Minister of St. Kitts and Nevis, sent me an invitation to attend a celebration on September 19, 1983. I accepted. This event marked the independence from Great Britain of the islands Nevis and St. Kitts (officially St. Christopher but nicknamed St. Kitts).

The Alexander Hamilton Museum, built on the site of his birth in Charlestown, was opening on Nevis the same day.

Parades, parties, and a concert/dance featuring Nevis-born musician, West Pemberton's band, New Horizons, were a part of the Independence Day Celebration on Nevis. At midnight on St. Kitts, Princess Margaret lowered the Union Jack for the very last time. Then the flag of the Sovereign Federal Democratic State of St. Christopher and Nevis rose into the dark night sky.

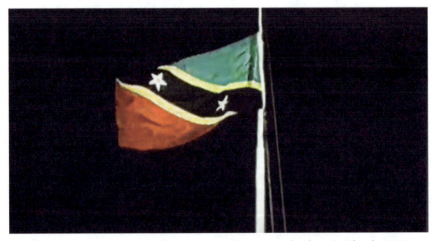

This picture shows the actual flag Princess Margaret raised on St. Kitts in 1983.

This signaled a new era for Nevis. Like the US, it was no longer under British rule. It seemed fitting that both the independence of Nevis and the establishment of the new Alexander Hamilton Museum, occurred at the same time and in the same place.

Alexander Hamilton was born on Nevis when it was under British rule, and he moved to America when the colonies were also under British rule. Technically, one could argue that he wasn't an immigrant then because he'd moved from one British settlement to another.

Nonetheless, it's an extraordinary coincidence that one of the most influential figures in the Revolutionary War victory, and in the creation and sustainability of the United States of America, was one and the same person. And he had been born in Charlestown, on the island of Nevis, in the West Indies.

 Laurens' List "B"
Prep School, College, Law 'School,' and War Accomplishments

This second *Laurens' List B* highlights Hamilton's education when he arrived in the American colonies. Included are prep school, college, law 'school,' and his subsequent military endeavors before, during, and after the Revolutionary War.

1. Island community leaders sent personal introductory letters with Hamilton to initiate his New York contacts.

2. He enrolled in grammar school in Elizabethtown, New Jersey in 1772.

3. Initially, he lived with the William Livingston family, and he possibly lived in other homes.

4. Receipts document that his cousin, Anne Lytton Venton Mitchell paid for most, if not all, of his education.

5. His accelerated study track request at College of New Jersey (Princeton), was denied.

6. He attended Kings College (Columbia) as a private (unregistered) student in 1773.

7. He registered as a Kings College student in 1774; initially he was interested in medicine.

8. He once told a friend, "I wish there was a war." If he were a war hero, he thought he'd gain honor and respect.

9. He prepared for war by reading books and receiving instruction on war techniques.

10. He supported colonial protests; he wrote pamphlets against loyalists' views in 1774 and 1775.

11. Sometime between late April and early May, 1775, he joined a militia, working so hard he was identified as a potential officer.

12. In March, 1776, he became captain of an artillery company.

13. After proving his patriotism, courage, discipline, military skills, and leadership, he was appointed to be one of General Washington's assistants, an official aide-de-camp.

14. A trusted war advisor, strategist, and partner, he was sent on military missions and fought in battles, including Trenton, Princeton, Germantown, and Monmouth.

15. He wrote Washington's correspondences, a task he shared with three other aides-de-camp. He wrote most, if not all, of Washington's extensive military reports.

16. Because he spoke and wrote French fluently, he was highly effective as General Washington's diplomatic representative to the French military command. (PERSONAL NOTE: Laurens lived in France from 1920 to 1930, so he could also write and speak French fluently.)

17. After a falling out with General Washington, Hamilton resigned. He stayed on temporarily due to staff shortages, and to facilitate a successor's transition.

18. He reconciled with General Washington after spending time with Eliza and his family.

19. General Washington finally gave him command of a New York Battalion, leading to the march to Yorktown.

20. In the Battle of Yorktown, he led troops on a successful assault of Redoubt 10 during the Revolutionary War's final victory. British General Cornwallis surrendered.

21. As a 'self-taught' law student, he studied in his father-in-law, Philip Schuyler's in-home law library.

22. Because of his war service, his law apprenticeship requirement was waived. He passed the bar exam in 1782, only six months after resigning his military commission.

23. In 1798, Washington chose him to create a 'provisional army.' He toiled diligently on army details in 1799.

24. President Adams secretly negotiated an end to the potential war. Thus, Major General Hamilton's 'provisional army' was disbanded. When Washington died in December, 1799, Hamilton became the US Army's senior officer until June, 1800.

25. In 1800, along with co-counsel Aaron Burr, he successfully defended a man accused of murder in the first US murder trial that had a full court transcript.

26. He created proposals for a military academy, similar to what became West Point.

27. Commissioned in 2014, the USCGC *Hamilton* WMSL-753 is the sixth cutter named after Alexander Hamilton.

CHAPTER 9
DESTINED DISTRESSES

Drinking, Thinking, and Linking

L et's step back about a decade.

When our financial holdings disintegrated shortly after we married, Laurens and I had gone from a life of luxury to struggling with downsizing everything. We broke the Lindwood Estate lease in 1967. After moving to a smaller house, we no longer needed a maintenance man. Or a cleaning lady. Mrs. B. retired and we'd already let Chief go, so I drove the Lincoln to go shopping and to pick John up from school.

Laurens had become more and more despondent and dependent on his scotch, smokes, medications, and crossword puzzles. He seldom left his bedroom. To keep supplies stocked, I began buying cases of scotch and cartons of cigarettes.

I also began feeling sorry for myself. I felt stuck, caring for my children and being a caregiver for an old man. In 12 years, we'd never been able to consummate our marriage because the little blue pills had not yet been invented. I wanted a loving husband like my friends had. I was extremely lonely so I began drinking some of Laurens' scotch. Soon, I was drinking more and more of Laurens' scotch.

Drinking helped numb me to some of the pain I was enduring. It also got me thinking…about things I had suppressed over the decades. That's what I was told to do during one of the biggest challenges of my life that began in the summer of 1948. *Forget **it** ever happened. Pretend **it** never existed.* My memories came flooding back to me one dreary afternoon when I was taking care of Laurens:

"It" actually began as a happy hobby in my pre-teen life when I learned to ride horses. My little sister showed a horse that was boarded at a stable owned by a family, whose 40-year-old son was a jockey. He had striking blue/gray eyes and was extremely nice to me. He asked if I wanted to ride the horses, too. Of course I did. I was a great rider and I had won many awards. He also offered me the opportunity to ride his horses in shows.

I was young. Barely 14.

I was extremely naive. I thought all people were good and had my best interests at heart.

I was very uninformed. My mother never mentioned sex and schools did not teach about it. I didn't even know about my period until my sister-in-law told me what was happening to me *after* I had started.

I was obedient, I liked to please people, and I was able to keep secrets.

That combination of traits made me a very vulnerable target.

I didn't know it at the time, but I was groomed to be assaulted. The stable-owner's son, ironically known as a stable "groom," knew I loved showing his horses. So he insinuated he'd find another rider unless I agreed to do certain things with him in the park, and later, in a back room of the stable. I was clueless. I just wanted to ride the horses.

In March of 1949, a month after I turned 15, I was not feeling well, so Mother took me to the doctor. By then, I was nearly five months pregnant.

When I told Mother about the horse groomer, she called our family lawyer and the police, who issued a warrant for his arrest. Mother did not want him to molest other children, so she wanted him put away. But that meant I had to testify at his trial. It was the most traumatic experience of my life.

In May, 1949, I was barely 15 years old, almost seven months pregnant, and I had to relive the horrible details of my attacks in a courtroom for the judge, lawyers, jury members, the press, and looky-loos—all total strangers. A few friends came to support me, but I was still mortified. Tears streamed down my face as I recalled those humiliating attacks. I told the truth.

"Your honor," the defense attorney stated. "As this young lady just testified, she was a consenting participant." *Oh my gosh, that was true. I did go along with his requests willingly...that was the only way I could ride in horse shows.*

The prosecution lawyer was adamant. "Your honor, first, she's not a young lady. She was only 14 at the time, so she is definitely a young girl. Therefore, because she was, *and still is*, not yet 16 years of age, she needs to be protected by the law." I relaxed a bit but the tears kept flowing.

"Furthermore," the prosecution continued, "under district law, sexual relations by an adult with a girl under 15, even a willing participant, is considered the same as actual rape."

What were all those big words? District law? Sexual relations? Willing participant? Actual rape? I just wanted to ride in horse shows.

"Members of the jury," the prosecutor turned to people sitting in a box. "This young girl just wanted to ride the stable horses. She trusted the groomer because, at age 14, she didn't know any better. You can stop this from happening to other young children. I ask you to return a verdict of guilty with a recommendation for the extreme penalty of death in the electric chair."

Through my tears, I saw Mother gasp and clasp her hands over her mouth. The death penalty? I knew she wanted him to be *put* away, but I didn't think she meant in *that* way.

Instead, he was sentenced to 23 years in prison. I was proud that Mother stood up for me and that justice was served.

My parents paid their hard-earned money so I could move to a private home for unwed mothers. Many activities and classes were offered to us, but the best thing I learned in my four months was how to type nearly 80 words a minute. Non-stop.

On July 22, 1949, I gave birth to a healthy 8 lb., 5 oz. baby, who was immediately whisked away to the hospital. They told me she was a girl but I never saw or held her. My parents paid a local Catholic Adoption Agency, hoping they could place my newborn baby with a good family. I didn't have a say in the matter. As far as I knew, I would never see her, hear from her, or know anything about her for the rest of her life.

And for the rest of my life, too.

That's why I was advised to *forget that **she** ever happened. To pretend **she** never existed.* They said it would be easier to get back to my normal life if I erased *her* from my memory.

Graphic details of the trial and my being a junior high school unwed mother spread throughout the local news channels and publications. It's no wonder that school boys took advantage of the opportunity to ridicule me. But it was their bullying that led to my hero punching one of them, sending him across the lunch table. Within a year, I had quit school as a senior, married my hero, Leo, and we had our own baby on the way.

In fact, we had five babies within 10 years, but eventually we grew apart. Leo moved out and we filed for divorce. Life got extremely difficult when I had to juggle childcare for five children with an evening job that kept me on my feet for hours at a time.

Then I met Laurens.

"Mary Anne?" As if on cue, Laurens called out for more scotch, interrupting my emotional tour down memory lane. After delivering his request, I kept on thinking....

Regardless of how brash and unexpected his declaration of marriage might have been, I believe that Laurens' entry into my life at that specific time was a godsend.

I had just been investigated for child neglect by the county welfare board. An unknown neighbor had reported that my children had been left unsupervised—neglected—during the evenings when I was at work.

When Leo and I first split, he came to the house during his evenings off to care for the children. Because he worked nights on alternate weeks, I also offered free room-and-board to a college student in exchange for her feeding the kids dinner I had prepared before I went to work. She also helped with homework, evening chores, and bedtime. She was Catholic and had been studying to become a nun, so as I expected, things went really well at first. But then I discovered that when Leo cared for the children, the student began staying out late with men. So I asked her not to come back when school was out.

By then the oldest boys were 13 and 14 in a state where babysitting was legal for 13-year-olds. Imagine my terror when I received that welfare board letter stating that a complaint had been filed. They needed to inspect my house, with only two days' notice, to see if it was acceptable, and to confirm that my children were well fed, well clothed, and well cared for. I was horrified.

Two days later, the investigator came and the report was written. The inspecting agent declared that our house was above reproach and that Leo, Jr. and Mike were doing an exemplary job making sure their younger sisters and brother were well cared for, were able to do their schoolwork, and went to bed in a timely manner. I was so proud of my children. And I was NOT a neglectful mother.

The entire confrontation was extremely grueling because the outcome was unpredictable. I could have lost my family while trying to provide for them. Can you imagine being in that state of mind two months later, when an elderly gentleman offers to pay you an amount equal to the same wages and tips you're earning, so you can stay home and care for your children?

Despite my initial hesitancy, I soon realized that Laurens was a godsend at a time when my life seemed to be teetering on a precipice. I was relieved that we'd passed the inspection and that our family could stay intact. But for how long? Thanks to Laurens, not only was our family together, but we were thrust into the midst of what some might refer to as a mythical life.

Part of that mythical life included Little League baseball when John was nine years old. I drove him to games early and then volunteered to help in the concessions stand with the other parents. As I had been doing for several years, I'd have a little nip of scotch before the game. But when the innings went on and on, I began looking for excuses to go back home for another drink. Whenever supplies needed replenishing, I offered to go get the items...and another nip of scotch.

One day, I realized that my drinking might cause me to say or do something that might embarrass or even hurt one of my children. It could happen at a game or at any kind of event. That's when I knew something had to change.

My parents' warning from my childhood flashed across my mind:
You made your bed, so now you must lie in it.
I decided I did NOT want to lay anywhere. I wanted to stand strong.

An *Ask Ann Landers* advice column suggested *Alcoholics Anonymous* so I found the nearest AA chapter in 1971. Amazingly, after I made up my mind to join, I stopped drinking—cold turkey—and I didn't drink a drop of alcohol for over twelve years.
Around 1983, many reasons to celebrate occurred, but I've maintained my status as an occasional social drinker ever since.

———◆———

1983 was a memorable year. We were living in Florida, Laurens had passed away, my children were all on their own, and I was only 49. My real estate career was going extremely well. I still reflected on my life's major challenges—being raped, giving up my baby, the ensuing trial, being a divorced-single-mom with five kids, the welfare investigation, and my excessive drinking—but I did *not* let them define me.

I realized I had many things for which to be grateful and that it might be time to give back.

Maybe I was destined to do something...
something no one else could contribute...
contribute some sort of a positive impact...
...a positive impact on the world.

I decided to take care of myself, focus on the future and things I could control, and move upward and onward. At the time, I had no idea that one day, I might be linking my life with historical events in a way that no one else on earth would be able to link.

In my quest to keep moving forward, I suffered a brief setback when I was diagnosed with breast cancer in 2021. Although we were in the midst of Covid 19 restrictions on in-person care, I took the same self-improvement steps I took in the '80s and am blessed to be cancer-free in 2023.

CHAPTER 10
KEEPSAKE DESTINATION

*My Contributions and a Major
Miscalculation*

Laurens had been so passionate about Alexander Hamilton's legacy that he displayed artifacts and mementos on our walls, shelves, and bookcases. I was just beginning to learn a few details about them when he passed away in 1978. He had given some valuable items to a few organizations, but we still had other keepsakes I knew about, including a pair of silver candlestick holders that had been owned by

Alexander Hamilton and his wife Eliza. We also had a rare gold coin with an embossed Hamilton's head image.

Laurens owned a three-foot lithograph of the famous Hamilton pose, standing upright with a hand on his desk. I gave the lithograph to the New York Chapter of the St. Andrews Society shortly after Laurens passed.

Portrait of Hamilton's best friend, John Laurens' father, Henry Laurens. Note: My mink stole was one of the many gifts I received from Laurens.

I also gave a three-foot portrait of John Laurens' father, Henry Laurens, to the New York Chapter of the Sons of the American Revolution (SAR). John had been Hamilton's best friend.

As mentioned, I was on Nevis Island in September, 1983, when Princess Margaret lowered the Union Jack on St. Kitts for the final night, ending British Rule for Nevis and St. Kitts. The official Alexander Hamilton Museum was opening on Nevis that same day.

My Journal: On September 19, 1983, I was invited to a special luncheon for Her Royal Highness Princess Margaret at Pinney's Beach Club at 12 noon.

Princess Margaret's Sixth Form College was at 2 p.m.

The Official Hamilton House Opening was at 4 p.m.

I attended all three events.

Cicely Tyson's parents had been born on Nevis, and Cicely was there to cut the ribbon.

Cicely Tyson spoke before the ribbon cutting. I'm in the front row (dark dress).

Commander Thompson, USCG, Cicely Tyson, and her family, the Honorable Premier Simeon Daniel, the Honorable Bertram L. Baker, New York State Assemblyman, and his wife, Irene, gathered in the courtyard.

Government delegations had come from as far away as New Zealand. Cicely Tyson gave a fine speech, but just as she was cutting the ribbon on the door, the sky opened. A deluge of rain moved the celebration inside.

I presented the new Alexander Hamilton Museum with an authentic pair of silver candle holders that once were owned by Alexander Hamilton and his wife, Eliza.

I also contributed a large gold colored coin with a Hamilton headshot embossed on it. The coin was encased in a black frame.

My candle holders were presented after Cicely's speech.

Later, I attended an Independence Day Cocktail Party at Zetland Plantation by the Honorable Simeon Daniel, Premier of Nevis, and his wife, Sheila. Although he has passed away, I enjoy being in contact with Sheila.

———◆———

After returning home to Seminole, Florida, I wanted to do more for the Hamilton Museum in Nevis. I now had a place to send any valuable historical mementos I might unknowingly still have. If I contributed keepsakes to places that appreciated their historical value, I could help promote Alexander Hamilton's legacy, just as Laurens had tried to do for so many decades.

Laurens gave a copy of his Hamilton portrait to the Society of the Cincinnati.

Laurens had an original portrait of Alexander Hamilton with an eagle medal. This exclusive piece was, and is, extremely valuable. He was so proud of this portrait that it was prominently displayed in every one of our homes.

Laurens commissioned an artist to duplicate this portrait in 1960. He presented the copy to the Society of the Cincinnati in Washington, DC. If you're like me, you might have thought of Cincinnati, Ohio, but Ohio wasn't one of the 13 original states. The Society of the Cincinnati has a unique history behind its formation and its name. This was Laurens' version of the legendary story:

The last major battle of the American Revolution at Yorktown was in 1781, but the war wasn't officially over until 1783. George Washington toiled with his fellow officers for six more years before becoming president in 1789. When he resigned in 1797, he shocked the world. No prior leader had ever willingly relinquished power once attained.

The officers all wanted to form an organization so they could stay in touch and preserve memories of their Revolutionary War accomplishments for all time.

About 400 BC, a legendary Roman Commander (and farmer) named Cincinnatus was recruited to win a battle because the Romans were convinced he would then relinquish power and return to his farm. He won the battle in record time and, showing his true virtue and character, he gave up power and returned to his farm. Washington had also resigned and returned to his farm.

The Army officers compared Washington to Cincinnatus. They named their new group the Society of the Cincinnati, vowing to follow the example set by Cincinnatus and their first president, George Washington. Both gave up power and returned to their citizenship.

The modern Society of the Cincinnati is the oldest patriotic organization in the United States. Membership is based on hereditary status: the oldest son, of the oldest son of the officers. Cincinnati, Ohio was also named after Cincinnatus, and, appropriately, is in Hamilton County.

I called the Society of the Cincinnati's headquarters in Washington, DC, to offer Laurens' original portrait of Alexander Hamilton with an eagle medal. My only request was that they send the copy of the portrait Laurens had given to them in 1960 to the Hamilton Museum in Nevis. They said they would, so I presented the original portrait to the Society in December, 1983.

I drove to Washington, DC in the winter to present this original portrait to the Society of the Cincinnati.

The copy still hangs at Hamilton's birthplace in Nevis. I also sent many first-edition books and pictures to Nevis.

***

My Journal: I was invited by the Premier of Nevis to attend the Annual Hamilton Tea Party to commemorate the birth of Alexander Hamilton. I accepted the January 11, 1986 invitation and asked my sister-in-law, Betsy, to accompany me. My brother, Ray, had passed away from cancer the year before, so I knew she'd love a trip back to the island. On January 9, 1986, we flew to Nevis.

Since 1959, Marion and William Trott have administered the Alexander Hamilton Educational Fund. This source provides for four Nevis-born students to receive Hamilton Scholarships. A fundraiser open house is held each year on Hamilton's birthday, January 11.

In recent years, the Lion's Club has assisted the Trotts in this undertaking. Americans who have recently participated in this affair include The Honorable and Mrs. Bertram L. Baker, former Representative in New York state. On Hamilton's birthday, Ambassador Robert Dubose was the guest speaker, and I read a poem Laurens had written called "Nevis Ode."

On January 13, 1986, the Nevis Historical and Conservation Society gave a cocktail party in my honor at the Alexander Hamilton Museum.

After the party, Betsy and I were dinner guests of Richard and Maureen Lupinacci at their hotel, The Hermitage Inn. As of 2023, Richard serves as the current president of the Hamilton Museum in Nevis. He and his family have owned The Hermitage Inn since 1971.

Built between 1670 and 1740, the Great House at the Hermitage is reputed to be the oldest surviving wooden house still in use in all of the Caribbean. The ancient cistern, water cooler and purifier, storehouse, and stone walls are well preserved artifacts.

The Great House was built with lignum vitae timber framing from Nevis trees, now extinct.

The entire property has been carefully restored as a charming public hotel. Additional buildings have been constructed or moved from other locations and refurbished at the Inn.

Today, The Hermitage is a plantation inn offering traditional island hospitality, original cuisine, reconstructed cottage rooms, a collection of antiques, old-fashioned gardens, horses, carriages, and local crafts and arts.

Betsy and I thoroughly enjoyed our visit there in 1986. We flew home on January 14 after spending five glorious days on Nevis. (More details on page 207.)

In 1990, I received a cordial invitation from the Nevis Island Administration to attend the Annual Hamilton Tea Party, commemorating the birth of Alexander Hamilton, on Friday January 11, 1991. The featured address was from the Honorable J. W. Parry, Minister of Agriculture. I accepted.

My friend, Peggy Lyman, invited me to stay at her home on Nevis. She was flying in from Texas, and, as planned, we arrived about the same time at the St. Kitts Airport. Her friends, Joyce and Michael King, picked us up and we stayed at their beautiful home that night.

The next morning we had breakfast with the windows all opened. Because there were no screens, little birds flew onto the table and helped themselves to the brown sugar. It was so delightful, something I'll always remember.

We went to the Hamilton Museum for the tea party, where the tables were set up in the courtyard with colorful tablecloths and beautiful flowers. Many people I had met on prior visits greeted me warmly.

———◆———

After I returned home on January 28, 1991, I sent a three-foot by three-foot, six-inch portrait of George Washington and his officers to the Hamilton Museum in Nevis as a gift from me. I really thought it was the final Hamilton treasure in our possession, but I was wrong in more ways than one.

Author Robert Thier once wrote, "Knowledge is power is time is money." I have a grand example of how much money might be squandered due to a simple *lack of knowledge* over a period of *time*.

Several years ago, I found a beautiful leather-bound collection of what looked like old newspapers. The letters "s" looked like letters "f," which made the documents hard to decipher. But they were all intact, well preserved, and had no tears or creases. I didn't make time to find out what they were. I just gave them to one of my sons.

One day, that particular son was excited. "Hey Mom, remember those old newspapers you gave me?"

The collection had been on the China cabinet bottom shelf for over 40 years. "Yes, why?"

He exclaimed, "I just sold them to someone on eBay for seven thousand dollars!"

"Oh really, that's good." I was happy for him, that is, until I discovered that the collection may have actually been an early edition of the 85 *Federalist Papers* that helped ratify the US Constitution. 51 were authored by Alexander Hamilton, 29 by James Madison, and five by John Jay. They are still relevant in present-day law. In 2021, an auction house in Chicago sold a similar copy for $175,000, and it could be worth even more today. We'll never know if it's the same copy we sold on eBay for $7K.

If I had made just a little bit of time to gain some knowledge, I could have added something extremely rare and enormously valuable to the Alexander Hamilton Museum collections. It's my sincere hope that the buyers appreciate what they have. I'll never forget that lesson learned.

By giving many treasured items to the Hamilton Museum and other historical institutions, I felt like I was helping to continue Laurens' passion for promoting his great-great-grandfather Alexander Hamilton's legacy. At the time, I wasn't aware of the depth of Laurens' reasons for his zeal, but it just seemed like the right thing to do.

One valuable Morgan family heirloom is a gorgeous portrait of Laurens' mother, Juliet Pierpont Morgan Hamilton, painted by Lena Mills in 1896.

Laurens' mother, Juliet Pierpont Morgan Hamilton was born in New York in 1870. She died in 1952 at age 82.

CHAPTER 11
DESTINED FOR REVOLUTION

*Musical Alters
Broadway...and History*

Laurens read many Hamilton books, including Gertrude Atherton's *The Conqueror*, a novel based on Alexander Hamilton's early years in Nevis and St. Croix, as well as his teenage and adult life, and his untimely death in 1804. After he discovered and promoted the 1902 book, Laurens hoped more people would become increasingly interested in learning facts about Alexander Hamilton. It became a bestseller in the early 1900s. His copy was so special that Laurens signed it to me and then gave it to me shortly after we met.

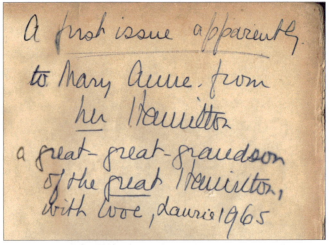

Laurens wrote: "A first issue apparently to Mary Anne, from <u>her</u> Hamilton, a great-great-grandson of the <u>great</u> Hamilton, with love, Laurie 1965."

After he died, I treasured his special gift, but eventually, I gave the book to a unique organization described later.

Laurens continuously tried to inform US citizens about Hamilton's contributions to our nation. He served in the New York State Assembly and, at the young age of 37, he co-authored legislation with Senator Feld that was named the Feld-Hamilton Law. It was the *State Employees' Career Service Law—the most progressive pay plan* (for everyday 9-5 workers) *ever adopted in any public or private jurisdiction.*

Although highly respected in the New York State Legislature and Civil Service administrations, Laurens was still unable to effectively promote Alexander Hamilton's legacy in a widespread manner.

Many, if not most of his speeches, were to audiences involved with the US Coast Guard (he was an Academy commencement speaker) and the New York Chapter of the Sons of the American Revolution (SAR, for which he served as president). He had been appointed to serve as a presidential commissioner, representing the Commonwealth of Virginia on the *Alexander Hamilton Bicentennial Commission* from 1956 to 1958. Laurens also founded the *Society of Friends for the Blind* on the island of Nevis, West Indies in 1957.

All of these organizations were associated with Alexander Hamilton by nature, but not all members had the same passion and appreciation for the depth of Hamilton's contributions as Laurens had.

Laurens was an Alexander Hamilton advocate with his other service organization memberships, including the Saint Andrews Society of the State of New York, the Army and Navy Club of Washington, and the Aramaic Bible Foundation, for which he served as chairman of the Board of Trustees. He was also a 32nd degree Mason and a member of the Committee on Electoral Reform of the American Good Government Society. Laurens continuously spoke about his great-great-grandfather's many contributions, but he was unable to generate the accolades that Alexander Hamilton deserved.

In 1964, Laurens' efforts were partially rewarded. The Honorable Bertram L. Baker (New York Assembly member 1949-1970), introduced a Joint Resolution to the Assembly, proclaiming January 11, 1965 as "Hamilton Day" in New York in honor of Alexander Hamilton's birthday. After serving as a member of the New York State Assembly from 1934 to 1937, Laurens was so well-respected that he was invited to the executive chambers as Assemblyman Baker's special guest. Governor Nelson Rockefeller signed the official "Hamilton Day" proclamation on March 16, 1964. Laurens felt honored.

The Honorable Bertram L. Baker was also involved in the issuance of the following resolution adopted by the New York State Assembly on February 23, 1978, shortly after Laurens passed away.

It read in part:

LEGISLATIVE RESOLUTION Assembly No. 129

Resolved, That this Legislative Body respectfully pauses in its deliberations and mourns the death of Laurens M. Hamilton, a distinguished former member of this Body, and extends its condolences to his wife Mary Anne Hamilton and his family members...

Resolved, That when this Legislative Body adjourns its proceedings this day it does so out of respect to the memory of our deceased colleague, the Honorable Laurens M. Hamilton...

I was astonished. The New York State Assembly shut down temporarily out of respect for Laurens' service after his death. He would have been as honored as we, his family, friends, and colleagues were by this incredibly respectful government action within only two short weeks.

The State of New York Assembly resolutions honoring both Alexander and Laurens Hamilton were a beginning, but they only impacted the state of New York. Laurens desired that the entire nation know what his great-great-grandfather's many accomplishments were.

Time and other contributors were still needed.

———◆———

When Laurens' wealth disappeared and his health declined, he seemed to give up on advocating for his family legacy. I had been to Nevis, witnessed many of the events, seen the evidence of multiple efforts, and experienced some of the tributes that honored the Hamilton family legacy.

But I was not aware of the depth of Alexander Hamilton's intrinsic contributions to our country's revolution, creation, foundation, and maturation as a nation. Even if I was aware, I could not continue Laurens' mission very effectively.

*Some**thing*** or *some**one*** else was needed *to continue it.*

Another Revolution.

That's what was needed to continue Laurens Morgan Hamilton's life mission and passion to promote his great-great-grandfather, Alexander Hamilton's legacy.

I don't believe it's a coincidence that, in 2016, the only man on earth who had started a Hamilton Revolution, Lin-Manuel Miranda, personally gave me a signed book he co-authored entitled: *Hamilton: The Revolution*.

On the second page of the book's introduction, co-author Jeremy McCarter wrote:

"The widely acclaimed musical that draws from the breath of America's culture and shows its audience WHAT WE SHARE DOESN'T JUST DRAMATIZE HAMILTON'S REVOLUTION: IT CONTINUES IT."

(Jeremy McCarter, *Hamilton: The Revolution*, April, 2016 ~ Used with Permission)

It's more than a *coincidence*. It's greater than *fate*. In my humble opinion, it borders on *providential*, and if Laurens were alive, I think he'd consider it a *miracle*. What the Hamilton Revolution has accomplished through the hit Broadway production *Hamilton, An American Musical,* **is continuing it!** It continues Laurens' mission in a miraculous manner.

The book is entitled *Hamilton: The Revolution*. It seems, however, that it could be describing not one, not two, but possibly three revolutions:

1. The American Revolution of the mid-late 1700s.

2. The Hamilton Revolution *about* the American Revolution.

3. The Broadway Revolution—First rap/hip-hop songs featured in a long-running stage production ever.

As I admitted in the first chapter, I initially thought rap and hip-hop were solely represented by what was booming and blasting from those cars that swayed past my house. But even in my 80s, I thoroughly enjoyed the production *Hamilton, An American Musical* in 2016. And if Laurens had been sitting beside me, I think he also would have appreciated every minute of it...in spite of the fact that he would've been 116 years old.

Why?

Because this phenomenon has accomplished in less than a decade what Laurens tried to do for more than 60 years. He focused mainly on older citizens but this production captivated and continues to attract multiple generations of audiences. And it extends beyond national boundaries, political parties, socioeconomic levels, ethnic heritages, cultural climates, and diverse lifestyles.

In my opinion, this production could also represent a fourth type of Revolution, one that reverses centuries of destructive 'legacy suppression,' like Hamilton suffered. Because he died so young, he couldn't defend his own legacy. Maybe label it as an *Anti-Suppression Revolution*.

For example, can you imagine what Thomas Jefferson, John Adams, James Madison, James Monroe, Aaron Burr, and other Hamilton detractors would think and say if they were sitting in the midst of a typical audience during an afternoon matinee of *Hamilton, An American Musical* in Anytown, USA?

In a fourth type of revolt—an *Anti-Suppression Revolution*—the critics, cynics, and disbelievers might say:

"We should have known he'd find a way to have the last word!"

Or, *"Burr silenced his mouth in 1804, but how does his pen keep writing after nearly 220 years?"*

And, quite possibly, *"We all knew 'He's never going to be president now...' but **now** people know that **he accomplished more** without being president than many presidents do during their entire term(s)."*

It'd be a very entertaining session. If it was a *Hamilton Sing-Along,* the hecklers might squirm in their seats to avoid the rapid-fire singing. That would be fun to see.

———◆———

One epiphany I received while enjoying *Hamilton, An American Musical* in 2016 involved my ability to fit Laurens' mission together with little-known aspects of American history. I began to understand more about

Laurens' frustrations with United States citizens who did not appreciate his passionate messages.

I also realized that education via the arts made the complexities of Hamilton's contributions truly come alive. The production had—and still has—the potential to impact all aged audiences from around the world because of its excellent performances, its historical messages, its diverse cast, and its many styles of music and dance.

Before the musical, most Americans only knew about Alexander Hamilton by one of three scenarios:

1. His portrait on the ten-dollar bill.

2. He died after a duel with Aaron Burr (the sitting vice president of the United States at the time).

3. 'Hamilton' was mentioned in a 90s era "Got Milk?" TV commercial involving a contest question.

Like Laurens, I want to help educate all Americans so they know more than three facts about Alexander Hamilton. Thanks to *Hamilton, An American Musical,* I was able to comprehend what Laurens had been trying to communicate for decades.

My passion is growing and I want "to continue it," to honor my late husband and his messages. I truly wish Laurens was here to see that this once obscured Founding Father—his great-great-grandfather, Alexander Hamilton—has finally received the national and global accolades he so richly deserves.

Many ask what Hamilton did to deserve credit and honor above the other Founding Fathers. After barely surviving the Revolutionary War, America was thriving within a few short decades, mostly due to Hamilton's financial structure and organization. In only a few years, his financial systems took the country from near bankruptcy to being on the road to prosperity.

During recent years, I've personally met a few people who wanted to know more than three things about Alexander Hamilton, starting as early as 2008. This was before Lin-Manuel Miranda's White House presentation during *An Evening of Poetry, Music, and the Spoken Word* event in 2009. It was also before the musical production *Hamilton* opened at the off-Broadway Public Theater and Broadway's Richard Rodgers Theatre in 2015.

As mentioned, after I experienced the musical in 2016, I was inspired to learn all I could about my great-great-grandfather-in-law's contributions as one of our nation's prominent Founding Fathers.

Laurens' List C highlights 40 facts, including Alexander Hamilton's family and how he and his wife, Eliza, directly and indirectly affected our nation's founding and growth, especially in the financial realm.

~~Laurens'~~ List "C"
Family and American Foundational Achievements

Although Hamilton left his Caribbean family, the following *List C* highlights his wife and their American family. It also features his multiple contributions to the creation, foundation, and maturation of our great nation.

1. In a 1798 letter to John Adams, General Washington wrote that Hamilton was his "principal and most confidential aid." After serving as an aide-de-camp during the war (1777-1781), Hamilton backed Washington as a cabinet member and as a friend until Washington's death in 1799.

2. In 1777, he met Elizabeth Schuyler briefly while he was delivering military correspondences to her father, General Philip Schuyler, in New York.

3. In early 1780, the Continental Army, General Washington, and his assistants—including Hamilton—were camped for the winter in Morristown, New Jersey.

4. Elizabeth (Eliza) was also in Morristown in early 1780, helping her physician uncle care for ill soldiers.

5. After reconnecting with Eliza at a dance, allegedly Hamilton was so smitten that he couldn't recall the company password when attempting to return to his quarters.

6. In December, 1780, he married Elizabeth Schuyler. Together, they had eight children and took in other kids. They raised a fellow Revolutionary War soldier's two-year-old orphan, Fanny Antill from 1787 to 1797.

7. In 1784, he defended a loyalist's rights because he believed in following the law, believed it would be good for America, and because it was the right thing to do. He was also known for defending the rights of other minorities, including freed slaves and Catholics.

8. Beginning in 1784, he set landmark legal precedents, including helping to create the judicial review doctrine.

9. In 1785, he became a charter member of the New York Manumission Society, to promote the freeing of slaves and to provide protection and legal assistance to free and enslaved blacks.

10. He represented the state of New York at the Annapolis Convention in 1786, where he called for a Constitutional Convention.

11. The Constitutional Convention was held in Philadelphia in 1787. He was elected to the New York State Assembly and was their convention delegate. His *Plan of Government* speech lasted for six hours.

12. He was the only New York delegate to sign the US Constitution. Nine states were required for ratification. All 13 states ratified, creating the United States of America.

13. As a member of the state ratification convention, he wrote 51 of 85 *Federalist Papers* between October 1787 and May, 1788. These essays promoted ratification of the new US Constitution and are still referred to today by attorneys, including the US Supreme Court Justices.

14. In 1787, he founded a group that became the first political party—the *Federalist Party*.

15. Appointed to his post as the first US Secretary of the Treasury in 1789, he developed President Washington's economic policies.

16. He founded the nation's financial system (public credit, the dollar, the banking system, the central bank, the securities markets, and the corporate system) which spurred robust economic growth that expanded middle-class wealth.

17. He was involved in the implementation of the US Executive Branch of government from 1789 to 1791.

18. He led the call for the federal assumption of states' debts amid intense Southern opposition.

19. He negotiated with Jefferson and Madison for the move of the US Capitol from New York to an undeveloped site along the Potomac River near Virginia, in exchange for their support of the debt assumption plan.

20. He established a national import-export tariff system to generate revenue.

21. He created the US Coast Guard to deter smugglers and to enforce the new tariff system.

22. He identified the US Postal Service as revenue to help pay off the national debt.

23. He was a founder of the Society for Establishing Useful Manufactures and the first planned industrial city— Paterson, New Jersey. He was the national driving force for US manufacturing, beginning in 1791.

24. He founded the First Bank of the United States in 1791.

25. He founded the United States Mint in Philadelphia in 1792.

26. He helped transform the US financial status from near bankruptcy towards prosperity within 15 years.

27. Foreign bankers studied and emulated his banking systems and financial foundations.

28. To protect the authority of the Federal Government, he and President Washington personally led forces on horseback to suppress the Whiskey Rebellion in 1794. They succeeded in securing 'spirits' excise taxes when the protesters fled.

29. He resigned from his Cabinet post in 1795 but remained active in political causes. Some call him the father of American capitalism. Others refer to him as the most influential cabinet member in US History.

30. He co-wrote *Washington's Farewell Address* in 1797, warning against the risk of excessive partisanship and factions.

31. He was a co-founder with Aaron Burr and others of a New York water service called the Manhattan Company in 1799. But he severed ties after discovering Burr's last minute secret charter clause, allowing the water company to transition into a bank.

32. In 1801, he founded the *New York (Evening) Post*, America's oldest, continuously published, daily newspaper. Unfortunately, the Hamilton's oldest son, Philip, 19, died in a duel defending his father's honor in 1801. His death was one of the initial stories covered by the *Post*.

33. Also in 1801, he hired an architect and a contractor to build a manor for his family in New York City. He named it The Grange.

34. Because Hamilton had put America's financial house in order, President Jefferson was able to acquire the Louisiana Purchase in 1803, doubling America's land mass. It also provided better access to shipping on the Mississippi River.

35. Hamilton died in 1804, in his late 40s, after an 'affair-of-honor' (duel) with Aaron Burr, the sitting US vice president. Due to his premature death, his enemies were able to destroy his unprotected legacy.

36. His sudden death left his wife, Eliza, and seven remaining children dependent on the charity of his friends. Hamilton had created and implemented intricate financial plans for our nation, but he left a debt-laden will and had no detailed estate plans for his family.

37. His friends established a secret account in one of the banks he had founded. This resource assisted Eliza and their seven remaining children, ages 2 to 20.

38. Their custom-built house underwent bank foreclosure procedures, but his friends helped Eliza repurchase it. She also petitioned Congress for Hamilton's military pension, which he had waived. She succeeded after 12 years in 1816.

39. Hamilton's contributions were ignored for centuries. Thus, he was dubbed the "Forgotten Founding Father." In fact, his image was nearly removed from the ten-dollar bill between 2013 and 2015.

40. Eliza lived 50 more years after Hamilton's death. She was very active preserving documentation of his massive writings and contributions, helping to establish a special free school, and co-founding an orphanage that continues serving children and families today.

CHAPTER 12
A DEVELOPING DESTINY

The Note on My Door

As I approached my front entry one spring afternoon, I saw something on my screen door. An envelope. Being a real estate agent, I was used to finding things like this, so I didn't think much of it. I brought it in and set it on the dining room table. But my curiosity got to me so I opened it. The typed message was different from any prior communication I'd ever received.

It read in part:

April 3, 2017

Dear Mrs. Hamilton,

My wife spoke with you awhile ago regarding real estate. Thanks for your input.... On another note, my friend and I are hosting a free family-friendly community festival for fans of Hamilton (the man and the musical)...and we would be honored to have you as a special guest to recognize your family's legacy. Please call me.

The note had a phone number, additional details, and was from a man named Greg. I didn't remember his wife but I called and was greeted by an exuberant voice.

"Hi, Mary Anne. This is Greg Plantamura. Thanks so much for calling me." He sounded very pleasant. "I am so honored to speak with you. I've been searching online for Hamilton information and was thrilled to see your story in the *Tampa Bay Times*. I have ultimate respect for your family's place in history. Thanks for calling me so promptly. I truly look forward to meeting you to shake hands personally. Thanks, again."

I was taken aback by Greg's passion for my family and our legacy. "You're welcome and thank you, too. I'm interested in finding out more about your program. You know where I live, would you like to come by?"

"Actually, my friend is a Hamilton fan who also lives in Pinellas County. Could we both come see you?"

"Yes, that'd be great." I was surprised that both of them lived so close. "How about next week?"

We set a date and time and I looked forward to their visit. I dug out my photo albums, filled a pitcher of ice water, and I was ready when they arrived.

A gentle breeze wafted in as I opened the door. Two men and a lady were smiling at me. "Mary Anne?"

"Yes…"

"I'm Greg and this is my wife Patricia. And this," he motioned to a tall man standing next to him, smiling broadly, "is Rand Scholet, founder and president of *The Alexander Hamilton Awareness Society*.

"Oh, HELLO! Please come in." Greg's friend's status and title surprised me. We exchanged pleasantries and settled in the living room.

"Thank you so much for inviting us." Rand set his briefcase on the floor beside him.

The cubes clinked noisily as I poured the ice water. "I'm so happy to meet you. It's amazing that you're all interested in Hamilton and you live in Pinellas County.

"We live just down the road," Patricia noted.

"My wife and I live a few miles north," Rand added.

I'd heard the word *Hamilton* but didn't catch the title. "I'm sorry I missed it. What's your society's name?"

Rand repeated the full title.

I'd never heard of it. "How'd this all come about?"

A sheepish grin spread across his face. "Well, it started over a beer and a dare."

I furrowed my eyebrows, unsure if I really wanted to know. "Okay…so what's the story?"

Rand leaned back. "I've been an IBM computer analyst all of my career and a self-professed 'history hater' all my life. I'm a numbers guy so I seldom read books…and if I read anything, it was for work, never just for fun."

My eyes widened. "You were a 'history hater' and now you run a history club? What changed?"

He leaned forward, resting his elbows on his knees. "My wife and I played coed softball and after games we would gather for drinks or dinner with our teammates at a local place. I don't drink, but one night, someone had a Sam Adams beer at our table. One of my teammates asked me if I knew who Sam Adams was. I told him 'I hate history so I have no idea.' "

My interest was piqued.

Rand resumed. "He got this challenging look in his eyes and he dared me to start reading his Sam Adams book. If I started it, he was certain that I wouldn't be able to put it down. I figured *Whatever, I'll read a sentence and then return his book.* "

"At our next game," Rand continued, "he brought me this big book on Sam Adams…."

I saw where Rand might be going, "And you finished it, right?"

"In one week," he smiled. "And then I went to the library and checked out more biographies about Founding Fathers' stories. I even bought books and started an office library."

"Incredible…" I marveled. "All because of a beer and a dare."

"Yes, it was," he continued. "I got hooked on stories about the early republic, the American Revolution, and the men and women who made it all happen."

Patricia grinned. "That's such an inspiring story."

"Yes, it is," Greg agreed. "But that's how Rand is, always interested in people and finding creative ways to help them pursue their goals, even if it means he takes an unlikely dare now and then."

I wanted to know more. "So, why Hamilton? Why the interest in my great-great-grandfather-in-law?"

Rand took a deep breath. "The analyst in me had to build a chart of the Founding Fathers' contributions towards creating our nation. So I made lists of most of their accomplishments back in the 1700s and compared the charts with how many aspects were still relevant today. I say most because I threw out the guys who seemed stuffy, or egotistical, or antagonistic. I then color-coded my chart."

Greg offered, "It's a great chart, you should see it."

"Thanks, Greg," Rand continued. "That chart is how I discovered I had no contributors on the subject of American finance."

I was shocked. "None? How'd you fill in the gap?"

"I had no choice," he sighed. "I dug into my pile of rejects, you know, the ones I'd thrown out. That's how I found Hamilton, prickly guy that he was. Turns out he'd created ALL of the financial foundations for our nation."

Rand became animated. "I couldn't believe it. In fact, I asked my daughter, who has a background in Political Science and Economics, if she knew about Hamilton's financial contributions. She only knew that his picture was on the ten-dollar bill."

His voice raised a pitch. "And she wasn't the only one. I couldn't find another person who knew much more than the ten-dollar bill aspect of Alexander Hamilton's life."

"Long story short," he took a deep breath, "I focused on learning all I could about him. After I discovered that his many enemies deliberately tried to wipe out all memories of him—and that he died before he could refute them—I decided to do whatever I could to reignite his diminished legacy."

I was captivated and wanted to know more. "How did you do it?" I wondered what secret he had that Laurens never discovered.

"I started researching and organizing everything on the web. I learned that in 2008, the National Park Service had moved and refurbished Hamilton's home he had built in 1801. They renamed it The Hamilton Grange and they were having an open house in New York City in the fall of 2011. So I went to New York, thinking I could contact masses of Hamilton scholars at this event."

It made sense to me. "How many did you meet?"

"None. Not one," he shook his head. "While I may not have met any Hamilton scholars, I met a couple, Tom and Mariana Oller, who had come to the open house seeking the same thing I sought—information about Alexander Hamilton."

Rand took a sip of water and continued. "We compared the Hamilton exhibits we'd seen and made small talk, but went our separate ways. When my wife, Cyndee, returned later, I wanted to introduce her to Tom and Mariana...if they were still there. Fortunately, they were." He sighed before continuing.

"We all began discussing the possibility of starting an organization to promote the Hamilton legacy. We were excited by our shared passion for learning about Hamilton and encouraging others to learn about him, too. So that's how *The Alexander Hamilton Awareness Society*, or *The AHA Society* was born. But it might not have happened if we'd missed Tom and Mariana after Cyndee returned. Of course, it took a couple years and many hours of talking, researching, and planning in 2011 and 2012 to really figure things out."

Rand then revealed an intriguing coincidence. "Some folks asked if I started the AHA Society because of the musical. Actually, I read Ron Chernow's book on Hamilton in 2008, about the same time Lin-Manuel Miranda read it. Being a writer, musician, and innovative genius, he was inspired to create the Broadway production, *Hamilton, An American Musical.*"

"With my analytical math and computer science background," he explained, "after I read the same book, I completed the flowcharts and Founding Fathers' charts* I'd started after the Sam Adams book dare. I'd dug into my rejection pile and found that our financial system was created by the same guy who later became the focus of the musical, *Hamilton*, which opened in 2015."

Others joined me in chuckling at the irony.

Holding up his hand to share another thought, Rand declared. "My wise wife, Cyndee, figured out that timing coincidence. She's very perceptive and creative, too. In fact, she coined the double meanings for our name, The AHA Society. Yes, we truly want to promote awareness of Hamilton's legacy and accomplishments. But we also hope people have their own light bulb "AHA" moments, like Hamilton often had.

I was intrigued. "What were your early activities?"

Rand recalled, "In 2012, we hosted our first Hamilton event at Trinity Church in New York. It went really well so we began hosting Hamilton events on the anniversaries of his birth, death and other milestone dates."

Taking a breath, Rand shared more. "In 2013, we hosted a 3-day event called 'Hamilton on the Hudson' in Poughkeepsie, New York. We chose the dates July 26-28 because it was the 225th anniversary of New York state's ratification of the US Constitution, which barely passed. Thanks to Hamilton's persuasiveness, the narrow victory was 30-27."

Rand continued. "Earlier, we'd learned that the same young man, Lin-Manuel Miranda, had created a musical tribute to Hamilton and was presenting what he called his *Hamilton Mixtape* at a Powerhouse Theater summer event at Vassar College, also in Poughkeepsie, New York. Just as we'd hoped, the mixtape actually debuted on Saturday, July 27, the same weekend as our 'Hamilton on the Hudson' events."

"Our AHA Society was still very new," Rand explained. "And we thought that having the *Hamilton Mixtape* event on the same weekend as our workshops might help more people become aware of Hamilton and what he did for our nation."

" 'Hamilton on the Hudson' had some great speakers and presentations," Rand stated. "The author of the inspiring book, *Alexander Hamilton*, was Ron Chernow, who participated in our Question & Answer session. And, as we all know, that partial *Hamilton Mixtape* developed into the musical *Hamilton*, which helped promote Alexander Hamilton's legacy in ways we couldn't have dreamed possible. After the show, I told Mr. Miranda—Lin-Manuel, what a great job he was doing."

"That's incredible, Rand," I responded. "Laurens would have been overjoyed to know others now share his passion and are taking action, not just talking."

Rand leaned forward. "Yes, Mary Anne, we were, *and are,* active. In early 2015, some of us went to the Public Theater to see *Hamilton, An American Musical* before it moved to Broadway. In fact, many of us saw it several times off-Broadway. After one of the shows, I congratulated Lin-Manuel again and we had our picture taken with a Hamilton "bobble-ham" doll."

Photo by AHA Society Vice President, Sergio Villavicencio

Rand with Hamilton creator Lin-Manuel Miranda at the Public Theater in 2015.

"Later, for the first Broadway show on August 6, 2015 at the Richard Rodgers Theatre, I bought 35 tickets—a fun expense to justify to my wife." He rolled his eyes.

"I invited all the folks I'd met who were involved with promoting Hamilton's legacy *before* the musical." He emphasized the word 'before' for obvious reasons.

"We were able to recoup *most* of that expense," he pursed his lips and shrugged. "But that was okay because I was so pleased to be able to provide that opportunity for everybody. We hosted authors, local leaders and others at a pre-show dinner and brought together many who shared our AHA Society's goal: Advocating for Hamilton."

"Amazing," I mused. Rand was doing exactly what Laurens had tried to do. But he didn't have the internet or the musical *Hamilton*. Two big reasons why he'd failed.

I turned to Greg. "How'd you discover Hamilton?"

He stated two words. "The musical."

"Me, too," I exclaimed. "He was my great-great-grandfather-in-law, so I should have known. But I didn't know the depth of Hamilton's contributions until I saw the musical. How'd you learn about the musical, Greg?"

"I'd heard all the hype about this new Broadway show," he replied, "and just didn't believe it could be that big of a deal. So I had to check it out. I got the cast-album CDs, and man, it was so great that when I played it in my car, I was happy even during traffic jams."

"That's what I found, too, Greg." I addressed them both. "So what are your plans with the AHA Society?"

Rand spoke with bursting pride. "In 2013, we officially submitted documents to the IRS and now, the AHA Society is an official 501(c)(3) nonprofit educational organization, serving as an open resource for factual, well-researched information on Alexander Hamilton and the Founding Era. We began planning and hosting celebrations on the anniversaries of Hamilton's life events in Florida, New York, New Jersey, the West Indies, and other places."

He continued, "We have a website with numerous historical resources for all ages. Some of our educational workshops are held in schools, libraries, and community centers as well as the Museum of American Finance in New York. We've had several presentations online, on C-Span, and on other television outlets. In fact, we helped lobby the Treasury Department to keep Hamilton on the ten-dollar bill. There's more, but that's the AHA story in a nutshell."

Rand turned towards Greg. "Tell her about 'Hamil*Fest.'"

Greg smiled. "I've hosted major events within the county before, so now we're making plans for a free Hamilton festival we're calling 'Hamil*Fest' at a local college. We don't have all the details worked out yet, but we are hoping you'll consider being our special guest, as I mentioned in my note. Is that possible?"

"It could be, but I'm just learning about Hamilton, too." I was honored but dubious. "There's a lot to study," I continued, "but I love meeting people and I enjoy speaking with groups."

"I'll help you." Rand sounded confident enough for both of us. I was glad to hear his depth of knowledge. "We have time to prepare and we can do this together. There could be many more events at other venues, too."

I wasn't sure what all was involved, but I said *yes*.

Meeting Rand, Greg, and Patricia was such a thrill. Greg was organizing a family festival, and Rand had started a new society. Laurens would have been ecstatic. He'd have been proud of me, too. I felt like I was on the verge of a whole new adventure in my life.

Rand and I with "Alexander Hamilton" at an exhibition in Philadelphia

I had a lot to learn, but Rand was a patient teacher. He'd been reading Hamilton books for nearly a decade when I met him, so he had quite a head start. We worked really well together, preparing for me to embark on educational engagements with him.

It was as if he became a Hamilton, too. In fact, I teased him by saying he could be a real Hamilton if he'd let me adopt him. That's the kind of relationship we had. I looked forward to taking our 'show on the road,' just like Rand promised.

Rand's Flow Chart descriptions can be found in his Seminole Historical Society presentation dated June 23, 2019. The link and QR code are on page 199.

CHAPTER 13
2017-2022 DESTINATIONS

My Hamilton Advocate Adventures

R and wasn't kidding. My journal reveals—in *italics*—the multiple venues we visited and the places where we spoke about Hamilton over the next four+ years.

NOTE: Some items are noted in shaded boxes and have more details posted in Appendix II (history) or Appendix III (stories). See Appendices I through III beginning on page 199.

Rand produced many PowerPoint presentations for our educational sessions. Because he was always exceptionally personable, he created relationships with people all over the nation and around the world. I was extremely blessed that Rand had made so many prior connections in his position as the founder and president of the *Alexander Hamilton Awareness Society.* In turn, he often told me that he also felt fortunate. Because I was a 'Hamilton-by-marriage' family member, my presence with him may have given us access to sites (and sights) that we might not have had on our own.

My Journal: On June 18, 2017, Rand and I traveled to Charleston, South Carolina, for the Change of Command Ceremony aboard the USCGC *Hamilton* WMSL-753. The officers posed for a photo with me.

I was honored by Captain Scott Clendenin, (me) Captain Mark Gordon, and Admiral Karl Schultz, USCG Commandant

We also visited *Mepkin Abbey,* the beautiful, family plantation where John Laurens was buried. He died in a skirmish after the Revolutionary War's major fighting was over. (More Mapkin Abbey details on page 200.)

In early 2018, my friend, David Downey, my neighbor, Vince, and I left for Nevis. On January 11, Hamilton's birthday, we met at the *Hamilton Museum* with the new Premier Mark Brantley, whose birthday was also on the same day. It was a bright tropical day and I was a guest speaker." *(See QR Code p. 199.)*

Premier Mark Brantley, David Downey, and I singing 'Happy Birthday, Hamilton' to Rand and friends in New York

We called Rand, who was in icy cold New York at *Trinity Church*, where Alexander Hamilton is buried. The US Coast Guard Auxiliary, dignitaries, and other guests were there, too, singing 'Happy Birthday to Hamilton' from freezing New York. Our group sang 'Happy Birthday' back to them from a warm and sunny Nevis island.

Rand singing, bundled up in New York

My daughter, Kitty, visited me in May, 2018, and I flew back with her to Maryland. Rand drove up a few days later and stayed with us. We toured the *Smithsonian* and saw the black marble wall by the escalators. My brother, Ray, had worked as one of the engineers helping to build the *Museum of American History*.

As we were leaving, Rand spotted a Revolutionary War uniform costume worn by Lin-Manuel Miranda in the musical, *Hamilton*.

Later, we went to the *Society of the Cincinnati* headquarters where we were taken into a private room. The staff took the George Washington Diamond Eagle out of the vault and we were able to view it up close. This medal is embedded with nearly two hundred diamonds, as well as several emeralds, and rubies. It was a gift from the French officers who fought with General Washington. He was the society's first president. After he died in 1799, Hamilton was elected president general of the society. (See page 201 for more details.)

Diamond Eagle Front Diamond Eagle Back

Two months later, my friends, Greg and Patricia Plantamura, and I flew to Newark, New Jersey. Rand picked us up on July 10, 2018 and took us on a historic sightseeing tour. In Elizabethtown, New Jersey, we visited the *First Presbyterian Church of New Jersey*, the old academy where Hamilton attended prep school in 1772 and 1773. We also toured *Boxwood Hall*, the home of Elias Boudinot, who was involved in revolutionary activities. Alexander Hamilton frequented *Boxwood Hall* while attending prep school.

We toured *Liberty Hall* in Union, New Jersey, the home of William Livingston, Governor of New Jersey. Alexander Hamilton lived with them when he first arrived in the colonies. He and Livingston's daughter, Kitty, were good friends.

At Paterson Falls, New Jersey, we enjoyed the visitor center, walked over to look at the falls, saw a statue of Alexander Hamilton, and noticed that a new larger visitor center was being built.

Ford Mansion – Washington's headquarters 1779-80. Pg. 202

Thomas Paine Monument (Common Sense author). Pg. 202

Jabez-Campfield House (Schuyler-Hamilton House). Pg. 202

Table Rock special stones and luxurious rooms. Pg. 203

Greg and Rand pose with a statue of Hamilton, "inviting" him to an AHA Society event.

We went to the *Morristown Green Park*, where life-sized statues of Alexander Hamilton, George Washington, and Marquis de Lafayette are exhibited together.

The next day, July 11, 2018, we drove to Tuxedo, New York, to see *Table Rock Estates,* where my husband grew up. Custom construction on the 40,500 square feet 52-room mansion began in 1900, with the cornerstone placed in 1904. Each of the 32 bedrooms had a fireplace. In fact, all 20 private bathrooms even had fireplaces.

Table Rock Estates, Tuxedo, New York, was one of the homes where Laurens lived as a child.

The horse stables and carriage house were converted to St. Joseph's Adult Care Home in 1942. The *St. Elizabeth Chapel* still serves valley parishioners.

St. Elizabeth Chapel is where many Hamilton family members are interred or buried.

We were met by the bishop at the *St. Elizabeth Chapel,* which was built in 1919, after the happy life of the Hamilton family was shattered by a tragic death. Eleven-year-old Elizabeth Schuyler Hamilton was a late victim of the 1918 flu pandemic. This beautiful house of worship was built in memory of Elizabeth, who is buried beneath the altar.

Laurens' mother, Juliet Morgan Hamilton, is interred in a crypt below the flagstone floor, as is Alexander Hamilton IV and his wife, Elizabeth Peltz Hamilton.

The walls have commemorative plaques for family members who were buried elsewhere, including my husband, Laurens Morgan Hamilton, 1900 - 1978. As mentioned, he had requested a US Coast Guard sea burial, which was officiated by the crew of the USCGC *Hamilton* WHEC-715.

The original Table Rock Estates spanned 2,000 acres in Tuxedo, New York.

Photo by Jump Visual

Early in the evening of July 11, 2018, we went to *Weehawken, New Jersey,* where Alexander Hamilton was shot by Aaron Burr during a duel on that same date in 1804. I met Douglas Hamilton, Laurens' distant cousin. Douglas is the 5th great-grandson of Alexander Hamilton. They are both descendants of Alexander Hamilton's son, John Church Hamilton.

The next day, we visited *Trinity Church* where Alexander Hamilton is buried. Many came to this event. (Hamilton's 1804 funeral had been the largest of its day.).

Rand and I spoke at Trinity Church on July 12, 2018, 214 years after Hamilton's death.

At Trinity Church, I gave a short speech about the time in January, 1966, when Laurens had taken me there to pay our respects and the groundskeeper had tried to keep us out...but we did get in. The New York chapter of the *Society of the Cincinnati* had donated a memorial plaque affixed to the wall. A large marble monument marks Hamilton's tomb beside his beloved wife, Eliza's grave.

The Hearts of Oak, a fife and drum reenactment group, played vintage Revolutionary War era music. Afterward, a group of *AHA Society* members had dinner at the *Fraunces Tavern*, where the Founding Fathers often met to plan and strategize.

We then went to the *Hamilton Grange*, the only home Alexander Hamilton built for his family. I was one of the *CelebrateHamilton* 2018™ event guest speakers. This time, the park staff was excellent, making up for our rushed visit through the mansion in 2016.

I enjoyed speaking to a group at Hamilton Grange National Memorial in 2018.

General Jedediah Huntington House is a historical home. Pg. 204
Mystic Harbor, has the oldest ship, built in 1841. Pg. 204
Slater Memorial Museum, Norwich Free Academy. Pg. 204

In October, 2018, Rand and I were invited to the *US Coast Guard Academy* in New London, Connecticut for an exclusive, special presentation, during the annual USCGA Alumni Weekend. This unique endeavor had been ongoing for five years.

We flew to the New Haven Airport, rented a car, and drove to Norwich to the *General Jedediah Huntington House*, a beautiful mansion built in 1765, and owned by Damien and Pam Cregeau.

I slept in the room where Lafayette had stayed. Damien told us that Hamilton never visited the Huntington House. I told him he could now say that 'Mrs. Hamilton slept in this room.'

(Left bottom clockwise) Rand Scholet, me, Nicole Scholet, Sergio Villavicencio, Bob White, Mariana Oller, and Damien Cregeau on the steps in the General Jedediah Huntington House.

The USCG Academy Class of 1963 celebrated their 50th Annual Reunion in 2013 and began considering a unique gift for the Academy. After contemplating many options, the class leaders and their special committee decided to honor

Founding Father Alexander Hamilton, the first US Secretary of the Treasury. They raised funds, secured permissions, met requirements, and commissioned an eight-foot sculpture to be presented on Alumni Weekend in 2018, their 55th graduation milestone.

Why Hamilton? In 1789, Congress approved Hamilton's plan to implement import taxes on "goods, wares, and merchandise, and on the tonnage of ships or vessels." The taxes were needed to pay off immense federal debts and to help fund operations of the new US government.

In 1790, Congress passed "an act to help collect the import taxes more effectually." The Revenue-Marine began with ten ships and it eventually became the United States Coast Guard, founded by Alexander Hamilton.

The sculpture project endured complications and delays, and the need to find a new sculptor after plans had been drawn. Research, construction, and casting can take years. But it was only 7 months before the unveiling.

Rand Scholet, founder and president of the AHA Society, referred renowned sculptor Benjamin Victor to the committee. After he was approved, Rand, and several AHA Society members helped research and contributed ideas for the sculpture's historical and artistic details.

As a result of combined efforts, the large-scale, figurative sculpture was completed on time and installed with two days to spare before the scheduled unveiling.

On October 12, 2018, it was raining lightly at the *US Coast Guard Academy* when we attended a gathering inside *Hamilton Hall.* I spoke about my husband's First Annual Alexander Hamilton Lecture on January 7, 1966. I showed the plaque given to him after the event.

Sculptor Benjamin Victor shared details of how he and Rand frantically raced the clock to finish in time. He thanked Rand for helping him complete the project.

Later, when the outdoor ceremony started, it was still raining. But as they unveiled the sculpture, the rain ceased, the sun emerged, and it was a gorgeous day.

We were treated to a regimental review—twelve hundred members of the Academy Core of Cadets marched in formations using a precise set of commands and close-order maneuvering. Patriotic music was playing

Rand and I with Benjamin Victor's *Hamilton* statue in front of Hamilton Hall at the US Coast Guard Academy.

as the sun brightened the sky. It was a grand day I will never forget. *(See QR Codes pgs.199 and 208.)*

The next day, Damien drove me to Wethersfield to show me his other colonial home, and then to the historic Cedar Hill Cemetery in Hartford, Connecticut. Included in this beautiful cemetery are the gravesites of such luminaries as Samuel Colt (billionaire creator of Colt firearms), actress Katharine Hepburn, and my grandfather-in-law, financier J. P. Morgan, and his family. It was comforting to observe Laurens' family's resting places for the first time.

━━━◆━━━

In 2019, my friend, Greg, learned about a Hamilton Tea Party on April 4 at the East Lake Library in Palm Harbor, Florida. Greg and I met Rand at the library to enjoy the event. To our surprise, the staff invited us to do an impromptu *Hamilton* presentation. No PowerPoint, no pictures, no photo albums—only stories and information. It was a wonderful session and they were an appreciative audience. In fact, it went so well they delayed serving the special teas until the end of the event.

After our impromptu presentation, Rand and I were served tea by the library host.

On June 23, 2019, I spoke at the *Seminole Historical Society. (See QR Code p. 199.)*

On January 15, 2020, Rand and I spoke for a *Sons of the American Revolution* (SAR) event at the Dunedin Country Club.

Rand and I greeted Admiral Karl L. Schultz,
Commandant of the US Coast Guard.

A 40th Anniversary Memorial was held on January
28, 2020, honoring the 23 US Coast Guardsmen who
perished when the USCGC *Blackthorn* WLB-391 was
involved in a 1980 collision on Tampa Bay near the
Sunshine Skyway Bridge. David Downey, Rand, and I,
attended the somber event on the Tampa Bay shores.

The permanent Blackthorn Memorial is located
at the rest area on US Highway 275, near the
north approach to the Sunshine Skyway Bridge in
southern Pinellas County, Florida. Until Rand took
me, I was not aware of the monument, but I highly
recommend visiting this peaceful park. It's open 24/7
for no charge.

On February 9, 2020, I spoke at the *Seminole
Library*, and Rand helped with a PowerPoint
presentation. My son, John, and his family attended.

After the 2020 pandemic cancelled public events,
Rand helped me do virtual sessions via Zoom. Covid
19 uncertainties made us wonder if this might have
been our last event together.

In early 2021, Rand found a writer to help create my book. I was busy during the lockdowns, writing my stories to continue promoting Laurens' family legacy. It has been a difficult but enriching experience, and I am inspired by the many people who have supported me.

Photo by The AHA Society

Benjamin Victor created another Hamilton statue that was unveiled at the *Hamilton Museum* in Charlestown, Nevis, on July 22, 2022, (which is also my daughter, Allison's birthday). I was unable to attend in person, but Greg produced my greetings on video and delivered them to the unveiling event for me. The YouTube video URL is: www.tinyurl.com/mah-7-22-22

 Scan QR code with your smart phone to see the video

As mentioned, please see more of my Hamilton Advocate stories in Appendices II and III (pages 200-208). I truly enjoy sharing them.

CHAPTER 14
DESTINY DISCOVERED

*When I Wasn't Even
Searching, It Found Me*

An event occurred over 70 years ago that still relates to my destiny today. I'll always remember this story:

> The cool evening breeze blasted through the opened door as the chattering Catholic University drama students swooshed into the Hot Shoppe diner. "Where is Mary Anne serving?" They always asked for me, their favorite waitress, so they could congregate in my section.

"I'm over here tonight," I beckoned. I was next to the bakery and scrumptious pastry aromas still filled the air. Although I was a teenager, the same age as many of them, I took pride in always providing great service.

A chorus of "hellos" greeted me as the drama players scooted into booths and scraped metal chair legs across the tile floor to get seated. "How are the boys?" They knew my husband and I had two small sons, so they tipped me extremely well.

"The little guys are doing great. Thanks for asking." I was always touched by their genuine concern...and their generous tips were a tremendous help, too.

Their university drama professor, Father Gilbert Hartke, was last to be seated for their post-rehearsal gathering. "Hello, my dear," he smiled at me. "I'll leave two tickets to our Saturday matinee at the will-call window for you and your husband, okay?"

"Yes, thank you so much." I made a note that I'd need to trade my Saturday shift and arrange for childcare.

Father Hartke always made sure we received complimentary tickets to performances at the Catholic University of America Theater in Washington, DC. As a practicing Catholic, the university shows had special meaning for me.

As with most teen-aged marriages, money was tight for us, so we had no budget for entertainment. These precious tickets afforded us the luxury of at least one evening out. We seldom missed a show.

Father Hartke made a tremendous impact on the entire community. In fact, a special outfit was given to him, while he was at the university, in gratitude for his contributions. The cornflower blue gingham pinafore skirt with a white top was no ordinary dress, but an exclusive heirloom, one of the only surviving garments Judy Garland wore in the 1939 classic film, *The Wizard of Oz*. Somehow, over the years, the dress seemed to vanish.

I served Father Hartke and the drama students in the early 1950s and, at the time, no one had any idea that he or Catholic University would receive such a historical costume in the early '70s. Nor could anyone imagine that in 2022, over 50 years later, the dress would be at the center of a national controversy regarding its ownership after being found in the university drama room.

———◆———

Similarly, the Alexander Hamilton family historical legacy was a national controversy that had been diminished for far more than a few decades. It had virtually disappeared. Our educational system's general history curriculum barely mentioned Alexander Hamilton for over two centuries. The destruction of the Hamilton legacy, however, had been an intentional effort, unlike the 'Dorothy Dress,' which merely had been misplaced.

Many ask how such a prominent Founding Father could have been forgotten.

1. Hamilton had many enemies—including four presidents succeeding Washington—who disliked him so much they destroyed his reputation and his subsequent legacy.

2. Hamilton was unable to defend his legacy because he died in his late 40s after a duel with the sitting US Vice President, Aaron Burr.

As mentioned, a resurging interest in our once-forgotten Founding Father developed after a 2004 book, *Alexander Hamilton,* was written by Ron Chernow. But none of this information would have been available were it not for the extraordinary efforts of many contributors who helped preserve primary documents.

The following people are at the top of most lists:

1. Hamilton's wife, Eliza, toiled for over 50 years to preserve his papers. She documented his war heroisms, confirmed his writings, and worked towards the inclusion of the Papers of Alexander Hamilton (PAH) into the National Library of Congress. Eliza's devotion—and her ability to forgive her husband's affair and other indiscretions—may have helped her succeed.

2. Hamilton's son, John Church Hamilton, organized his father's primary documents and wrote the first Hamilton book around 1834 entitled *The Life of Alexander Hamilton.* He then wrote a series of books that were not published until after his mother passed away in

1854. I had this series but gave them to a St. Petersburg attorney named John Wallace Hamilton in the 1980s. I'd like to contact his family to confirm they know the value of these books. *(Please see page 208.)*

3. In the late 1890s, author Gertrude Atherton self-financed a research trip to the West Indies and helped preserve records of the Hamilton family's early years. She then wrote a historical fiction novel based on Alexander Hamilton's life entitled *The Conqueror*, which became a bestseller, possibly because of her extensive research. This 1902 book inspired my late husband to learn more about his great-great-grandfather.

How does this help me find my personal destiny? I digress a bit to explain.

I know what it's like to lose something of value, seemingly forever. Sometimes, things perceived to be lost permanently might then appear to have even more value when found.

- The 'Dorothy Dress' had been misplaced in the Catholic University drama room, but was found in 2021.

- The Hamilton Family legacy had been denigrated, but interest was reignited via the arts in 2015.

- I gave away my baby girl in 1949 when I was only 15 through a Catholic Agency closed adoption.

All three scenarios may seem to be different but they could produce similar results, as illustrated in the following true story, which happened to me in the 1980s.

The call of a blue jay and the warm Florida sunshine flowed through the open kitchen window that February morning in 1983, as I prepared to meet a real estate client. When I opened the door to leave, the phone rang. I paused briefly but decided to let my brand-new answering machine record a message. For some reason, I stopped. As if a magnet was pulling my feet back, I was suddenly close enough to reach for the receiver.

"Hello?"

"Are you sitting down?"

I recognized my cousin Elaine's voice.

Thoughts of my real estate client's appointment flew out the open door as I pulled up a chair. *What did Elaine have to tell me that might be so shocking that I'd need to be sitting down?*

I finally responded. "Yes, I am. Why?"

"My daughter got a phone call from a young lady who was born in 1949 and wanted to know if I was her mother. But I would have been twelve back then so...." Elaine's voice trailed off, waiting for my reply.

"Oh really..." I was surprised, but because I have such a laid-back personality, I waited.

Elaine continued. "My daughter gave me her name and phone number. She offered to 'cease and desist' if you don't want to be found. But if you want to call her, here's the information."

I wrote down the name and phone number and thanked Elaine for calling me. It had been 33 years since my baby had been born at the maternity home's birthing room and then quickly whisked away to the adoption agency's hospital. My mind started to swivel with a myriad of emotions: shock, disbelief, anticipation.

I was glad I was seated as I stared at what I had written down.

Allison.

So that's what her adoptive family had named her.

My eyes closed and I let my memories wander back to the day that she was born during the summer of 1949. I knew there was no way I could keep her, so that thought was never a possibility. I had no say in the decision. Even though it seemed like I had lost contact forever, I still wondered about her every July 22, which was also Rose Kennedy's birthday.

A brisk breeze flowing through the window jarred me back to 1983. As I gathered my purse and brief case and started toward the door to meet my real estate client, I wondered how Allison had found Elaine's daughter. So I shut the door, sat back down, picked up my phone, postponed my appointment, and called Allison.

"Hello?"

"Allison?" It was surreal hearing her voice for the first time.

"Yes?"

"I can hardly believe it," I stayed calm. "I'm your birth mother, Mary Anne. My cousin Elaine said you contacted her daughter. I'm really happy that you did."

"Oh! Hellooo! I'm so glad I finally found you. I've been hoping and trying for years." She sounded relieved. "Thank you so much for calling me back. I've been wondering about you since my parents told me I was adopted."

We both had many questions, but I started. "How'd you find me?"

Allison explained, "A long time ago, my adoptive mother had papers that my adoptive father had been saving for me before he died, but she didn't give them to me until recently. They included my original last name, Eichhorn, and a Catholic Standard newsletter with a wedding announcement and photo of someone named Elaine Eichhorn. My adoptive father thought Elaine might be my birth mother."

My mind started whirling back over the decades.

Allison continued, "I called the church where the wedding was held. It had been years, but the church secretary remembered the newsletter article and photo because, get this, it had two errors she'd made on both the wedding location and the groom's last name. Amazing, isn't it? She gave me the correct last name of Elaine's groom. So I dug through all the phone books at the public library, and I finally found a number."

Allison quickly took a breath but I was anxious. "So what happened?"

"I called, but the person who answered was very confused, and didn't think her daughter-in-law had had any prior children. She was not helpful. I was disappointed but I couldn't give up."

"What'd you do?" I was impressed by her determination.

She resumed. "One day, I told my best friend what had happened. I showed her the picture with the groom's correct last name, and she goes, 'Oh, I know him, he's my boss.'"

I was too stunned to speak.

Allison wasn't finished. "My friend's boss called their daughter and gave her my contact information. Their daughter told her mom—your cousin, Elaine—who then called you. That's how I found you. I still can't believe it."

"What?" I was confused at first but it finally began to sink in. *Allison's best friend's boss was also my cousin, Elaine's husband!*

She continued. "I was a competitive swimmer and some of our swim meets were televised. I have a large mole on my back so I hoped there might be a chance you'd recognize me if you saw my mole."

"Oh honey, I never even saw you. They said it would be better if I didn't hold you. They just took you away." To think that she'd been hoping I'd find her all these years.

I was so happy I couldn't quit smiling. "I've been thinking about you every July 22nd for the past 32 years. Thank YOU for never giving up. Let's get together soon." We talked about the decades we'd lost, and I was grateful that we would soon be reunited.

Coincidence? Providential? Miracle? I believe it was all three...and destiny, through a Catholic church newsletter containing double errors that helped the church secretary remember it. Then she was able to confirm Allison's best friend's boss's correct last name!

Allison brought her son and twin daughters to Florida to meet me in June, 1983. Immediately I noticed her striking blue/gray eyes, just like her father's. (By then, he'd completed his prison term and eventually, she found him, too.) Allison's twin girls' birthday is June 2, the same day as my son Leo's. Coincidentally, Leo has twin sons, too.

Mother lived nearby, so Allison and her children got to meet her. Thus, they were able to appreciate what a remarkable person she was.

My mother, Nelia Rice was an extraordinary woman. She'd been so helpful before Allison was born, but her accomplishments began way before I was born.

In 1918, Mother was engaged to Ray Eichhorn, who suddenly enlisted in the Army and was sent to Europe. A friend talked her into joining the US Naval Reserve, giving her something to do until he returned.

Mother and her friend were among the first women allowed to join the US Military—outside of the nurse corps. Female sailors were known as Yeomanettes and only assigned clerical tasks. This was two years before women could vote.

After Ray returned, they were secretly married on February 8, 1919. (She wasn't sure if the Navy would allow her to get married, so she didn't ask.) She was honorably discharged on July 31, 1919. They raised us four children and were married until he died in 1956.

After 26 years of service with the Federal Government Accountability Office (GAO), Mother retired in 1960 but remained extremely active. She remarried in 1960 and again in 1968, but both men passed away. My resilient mother had outlived three husbands.

Mother moved in with me in 1984, and I was privileged to care for her during her final years. After her stroke in 1992, I visited her daily at the V.A. Hospital. A year later, she was discharged and moved home with me.

In 1994, Mother passed away only five days short of her 96th birthday. She was buried next to my father in Arlington National Cemetery, just down the hill from President John F. Kennedy and his wife, Jackie.

I was so glad Allison and her children got to meet Mother in 1983. We had a wonderful time together at Busch Gardens, Disney World and at the beach, and our entire family kept in contact over the years.

After 33 years, I was reunited with my daughter, Allison, and I met her three children, my grandchildren, for the first time. This picture was taken at Busch Gardens in June, 1983. L-R: Khalil, Allison, Mona, and Resna (twins).

CHAPTER 15
DESTINED CONCLUSION

*Laurens' Legacy Gives Me a
New Lease on Life*

Discovering my personal destiny involved choices, chance, and unique coincidences. It would seem unlikely that a 14-year-old, unwed rape-survivor—who testifies at a trial that sends her attacker to prison for 23 years, who gives up her baby at 15, who marries at 16, and, who becomes a struggling waitress and soon-to-be-divorced mother of five children, ages 4 to 14—could actually make a date with her historical destiny at age 31.

But that's what began in 1965, when Laurens Morgan Hamilton courted me *and* my five children. And that's what happened in 1966, when I married into Alexander Hamilton's family.

After all I had overcome, it had to be more than a series of coincidences that suggested I was destined to be a Hamilton. Some may call it providential or miraculous. But if an iconic dress can be lost and then found, if a family legacy can be destroyed and then restored, and if a birth mother can be reunited with her birth child after 33 years, then it is my opinion that my destiny can be defined by one decision that led to my second wedding in 1966.

My remarriage changed everything for our family. But I wasn't aware of the magnitude of my choices until Monday, April 11, 2016—50 years later—when I witnessed *Hamilton, An American Musical* at the Richard Rodgers Theatre in New York City.

I knew that my late husband had tried to attain the accolades deserved by his great-great-grandfather. But until that night on Broadway, I had no idea about the enormity of this specific Founding Father's contributions to the establishment of our country. I finally began to understand, thanks to the genius of Lin-Manuel Miranda, and the magnificent *Hamilton* musical he created.

The show was so inspiring that it helped me realize my providential destiny:

To continue my late husband's passionate mission as a Hamilton advocate, promoting awareness about my great-great-grandfather-in-law, Alexander Hamilton, and the monumental contributions he made towards the creation and sustainability of our nation.

In short, my destiny is to promote the mission of the *Alexander Hamilton Awareness Society*, founded in 2011 by my dear friend and confidant Rand Scholet. He inspired me in my twilight years to continue my late husband's quest by being a local, regional, national, and global ambassador for Alexander Hamilton's legacy. Becoming a Hamilton advocate gave me a whole new lease on life when I was 82 years old.

That's why I agreed with Rand to have another friend—and fellow AHA Society member—help me write this book. It's why I inserted specific Hamilton facts between stories. The basic truths on *Laurens' Lists A, B, & C,* are the reasons why this memoir is so important.

Rand | Mary Anne | Helena
Scholet | Hamilton | Reynolds
Bradenton, Florida ~ 2019

During our many educational sessions from 2017 to 2020, Rand and I could walk into a room and make instant friends. We were a great team, even after he stepped down as the AHA Society president in 2019 and the board elected new officers. He continued serving as a board member and he took me everywhere with him.

Rand and I wore our AHA Society Alexander Hamilton tee-shirts to our sessions.

Unfortunately, Rand passed away suddenly on July 29, 2021, at age 64. I miss him tremendously. The impact he had on my life had helped me overcome a difficult time in the summer of 2017 when my son, Michael, 64, and daughter Anna, 60, both passed away.

Rand may be gone, but his mission lives on through the AHA Society, the musical, *Hamilton*, my book, and the efforts of other family members and unrelated authors. Hopefully, this book will help continue Laurens' *and* Rand's quest to inspire everyone around the world to seek information about Hamilton's lifetime contributions.

I believe that knowing who Hamilton was, what he did, and the ensuing results of his efforts, will help people from all over our great country (and around the world), appreciate the precious freedoms and amazing opportunities he helped create for all of us. *Thus, such freedoms and opportunities can be preserved for an unlimited number of generations to come.* This was, and is, my driving passion and it's shared by my co-author as well.

Other creative ideas have been produced by multiple presenters all around the nation to encourage people to learn about Alexander Hamilton's accomplishments. Here are a few samples:

CREATIVE IDEAS - One Day Events

One of the first events I attended with Rand was *"Hamil*Fest,"* the full-day celebration Greg had invited me to on the first day he, his wife, and Rand visited me. It was held at a college in St. Petersburg, Florida. My son, Leo, arranged for the Admiral Farragut Academy band to provide the opening music. Students of all ages brought their parents and grandparents, and many young people asked excellent, relevant, historical questions.

The county-wide event featured sing-alongs, costume and talent shows, dance performances, prizes, tea duels, fan panels, themed mini-golf, and vendors. I was a guest speaker, along with Rand and others.

Rand observed that instead of parents dragging their children to a historical event, many kids were bringing their parents. Some students knew more about Hamilton than their teachers did. Students, teachers, and parents were all enthusiastic learners and participants together.

I thoroughly enjoyed these events because of the educational opportunities the young people were excited to be a part of. They stood in line, sometimes 20-30 people long, to ask me questions and have their photo taken with me. Who would believe that a woman in her 80s could command such attention?

Today's youth are interested in our nation's history. Knowing who Alexander Hamilton was, and what he did in the past, positively impacts our lives today.

CREATIVE IDEAS - Weekly On-going Events

Rand supported an elementary teacher in the Midwest who started a Hamilton club that met after school. The teacher described the club as follows:

*This was a weekly gathering of **HamilFans** and history lovers who share a love for digging into history and applying its lessons to today. We met for an hour and a half each week, for six weeks. I had two sessions each school year and did this for three years.*

The central focus of our sessions was Alexander Hamilton, the man and the musical. Each week we started with a game, a hands-on challenge, or scavenger hunt. We then analyzed lyrics, read primary documents, and sometimes we got to chat with historians, actors, and leaders involved with Hamilton.

We also watched a performance of some clips from the musical (this was 2017-2019 so we didn't have it on Disney+ yet). As a group, we supported local youths aging out of the foster system as a way to honor Eliza's legacy. She co-founded the New York Orphan Asylum Society, now known as Graham Windham, a private nonprofit in New York City, still serving children and families today.

Culturally speaking, we posed the question, "What is Hamilton's impact on popular society today?" Three examples from my elementary school-aged students were as follows:

* Hip-hop, as an art form is widely accepted in mainstream.

* Awareness of the need for stages to reflect America today in all its diversity.

* Lin-Manuel Miranda, Hamilton's creator and star, is an agent for change, equity, and justice.

CREATIVE IDEAS - Monthly On-going Events

I've heard stories of other Hamilton fans seeking information. On the West Coast, one lady tried to find adult educational workshops on Alexander Hamilton because she'd listened to both of the

Hamilton sound-track CDs while reading the lyrics. She learned so much about our nation's history that she wanted to know more. Her local theater educational director informed her that there were *Hamilton* educational opportunities for students in schools meeting specific guidelines, but nothing at the time for adults. A suggestion was made. "Why don't *you* start something for adults?"

So she did.

In 2016, she organized, advertised, and hosted monthly educational and entertaining sessions she called **Hamilton Discussion Groups.** These involved the *Hamilton* musical soundtrack and the book *Hamilton: The Revolution*, (both by Lin-Manuel Miranda, the latter co-authored by Jeremy McCarter). Various websites displaying song lyrics were projected on the wall. Her organization paid royalties for public performances to ASCAP, BMI, and SESAP, fulfilling the fee requirement for playing CDs at a public community center.

The participants, men and women, aged 40 to 90, read and discussed the lyrics to all 46 Hamilton tunes, three to four songs every month for a year. The discussion leader read the footnotes of stories and anecdotes related to songs from the *Hamilton: The Revolution* book. After a Q & A session, the group heard the entire song while the lyrics were simultaneously projected on a wall.

I was a Hamilton Discussion Group guest via speakerphone and Zoom in 2018 and 2020. It was fun sharing my stories and they appeared to like them, too.

According to the organizer, many members later stated that their Hamilton Discussion Group involvement greatly enhanced their ability to enjoy the live production and musical movie. Sometimes, they were even able to assist others who had difficulty understanding the fast-moving lyrics. I loved hearing such stories of educational benefits for audiences of all ages.

I love speaking with all aged Hamilton fans, one-on-one or in a group. This photo was taken at Weehawken, New Jersey on July 11, 2018.

###

OTHER CREATIVE *HAMILTON* INSPIRATIONS

A Cabinet Election Adventure

A friend from the Northwest told me about her special-needs grandchild who was intrigued by Alexander Hamilton after seeing the movie version of *Hamilton, An American Musical* on Disney+. The grandchild and a parent then enjoyed the live production at a local theater and now this student is excited about Hamilton and history.

When Associated Student Body (ASB) officers were being elected at the local middle school, this special-needs student created a campaign for school elections, made posters, wrote a speech, recorded a video, and was asked by other students to pose for selfies beside a campaign poster. Incredibly, this student won the election in a landslide over four other office-seekers for ASB Vice President!

The Election of 1800, a song from *Hamilton*, was extremely inspiring to this student, who was proud to be an official cabinet member, serving with other elected student officers. Although it was on a much smaller scale than during Hamilton's era, being a school cabinet member was a great, educational experience in leadership.

Many other special-education and general-education scholars were—and are—motivated by *Hamilton, An American Musical* to learn about history, too.

###

OTHER CREATIVE *HAMILTON* INSPIRATIONS

An Alternative Historical Literary Adventure

A friend from Texas, Lewis Smith, created an inspiring alternative history novel in 2021 entitled *President Hamilton.* This excerpt is from his book:

On July 11, 1804, a single bullet changed the course of American History. But what if it didn't?

Alexander Hamilton lies wounded and feverish after a deadly duel that ended the life of Vice President Burr. Hovering near death, he catches a glimpse of what lies ahead—and sees a Civil War that will consume a generation and poison America's future. His vision compels him to return to the political arena.

He sets his eyes on the Senate, and then the White House, enlisting former allies and reconciling with old enemies in his quest to become President and crush slavery.

Overcoming great odds while facing down enemies at home and abroad, Hamilton moves steadily toward his goal—but there are some who will stop at nothing to derail the President's crusade for liberty. Will they succeed?

President Hamilton: A Novel of Alternative History
by Lewis Ben Smith, (www.electiopublishing.com)

I urge all to read this book. Although it's fiction, it is a look at "what might've been and what still could be."

###

CONCLUSION

These and many other stories provide me with inspiration for writing this book. I truly want people of all ages, all ethnicities, all socioeconomic levels to appreciate our national heritage. For me, Alexander Hamilton represents more than just being my great-great-grandfather-in-law. His legacy was disparaged for far too long. I want to continue the mission started by my late husband, Laurens, and my friend, Rand:

Promoting education of the Alexander Hamilton Family Legacy with the goal of uniting our nation in a way that would make Alexander proud.

Sources reveal that some of Hamilton's final words in the summer of 1804 were: "If they break this Union, they will break my heart." I want this book to help heal the hearts of all our country's citizens so that we can continue to be one of the greatest nations in the world, a place where people want to live without partisan divisions, working together for the betterment of the UNITED States of America.

The main reason I was motivated to write this book was, as I've mentioned, because Lin-Manuel Miranda's Broadway phenomenon, *Hamilton, An American Musical* inspired me to learn about my great-great-grandfather-in-law. Hopefully, this book helps share that knowledge with people of all ages around the world.

An additional reason I wrote it is because many friends—and even mere acquaintances—who have heard some of my stories, have said that various aspects of my life *seem almost mythical.* I've often heard people say, "You should write a book."

So I did…with a little help from my friends.

I've mentioned going to Catholic Mass every Sunday, attending private Catholic schools, and placing my baby through a Catholic Adoption Agency. I may never know how or why, but I've always felt like I've had an 'Angel on my Shoulder,' guiding me, protecting me, defending me, and looking out for me… all of my life. This is another reason why I believe I was destined to be a Hamilton.

In closing, I'm hoping my efforts will inspire all readers to seek additional information relating to Alexander Hamilton, the vision he had for our nation, and how his ideas can impact your life. I truly hope *you* can find your own destiny and enjoy the same purpose and satisfaction in living that I have.

Mary Anne Hamilton

ACKNOWLEDGMENTS

This memoir and educational project began as a joint venture with Rand Scholet, a few months before he suddenly passed away. His wife, Cyndee, shared many informative facts, as did Tom and Mariana Oller, Chair and Vice-Chair of the Alexander Hamilton Awareness Society Board of Directors. Early supporters were Greg Plantamura, creator of Hamil*Fest, a free family event, and Lewis Smith, author of *President Hamilton*. Barry Zito's book *Curveball*, with its educational "Barry's Basics" (baseball facts), inspired our "Laurens' Lists" (Hamilton historical facts). We, too, listed facts between stories.

Editors Veronica Hartman, Barbara Kindness, and Mariana and Tom Oller spent tireless hours working to improve our manuscript. We appreciate their incredible contributions.

Michael E. Newton, author, and historical research expert, helped confirm our "Laurens' Lists." David Downey, USMC, and active with the USCG, supplied military resources. Also supportive were Nicole Scholet, President of the Alexander Hamilton Awareness Society (the AHA Society); Sergio Villavicencio, Vice-President of the AHA Society; Pam and Damien Cregeau, historical consultant, and American Revolution scholar; and Richard Lupinacci, president of the Hamilton Museum in Nevis.

We are grateful for business and art assistance from Richard Battershell, CPA, Battershell and Nichols; Dianne Durante, author, and art historian; Vince Post, Jr., retired bank administrator, and former theater board member; Ted Staff, WA State DoR; and Jason Reynolds, graphics designer.

Other contributors were Jocelyn Sladen and Wendy Arundel, daughter and granddaughter of Laurens' best friend, Russell Arundel; Lynn Gostwick, marketing director of Trinity Church, New York; Doug Hamilton, President, New York Chapter of the Society of the Cincinnati; Diana Seamon, elementary teacher and Hamilton enthusiast; Benjamin Victor, sculptor, Benjamin Victor Studios; and Sister Michele Yakymovitch, St. Joseph's Adult Home (Table Rock), Tuxedo, New York.

General support was appreciated from Pastor Jeff Hamling, Trinity Church, Montana; Marisol Sanchez-Best, Director of Education, Seattle Theatre Group; Sharon Gentry & friends, Curves gym, Federal Way, WA; and Sara Elisa Miller, Director of Philanthropy, 5000 Broadway Productions/Miranda Family Fund.

We are grateful to our manuscript readers for their interest: Sue Anagnos, Debbie Bowie, Janet Fix, Barbara Kindness, Karen Kingsbury's staff, Alysia Klugow, Erik Korhel, and Traci Stewart. Their input was encouraging.

Our families—children/grandkids—have been supportive and we appreciate their patience: Leo and Brenda Clark, Kitty Clark Wright, John and Jackie Clark, Allison Hairston, Dave, Jana, Jason, and Julie Reynolds.

We're indebted to all who helped us on this journey. Thank you. We hope our readers are entertained, inspired, and educated because of our combined efforts.

APPENDIX I
Family Resources and Links

The Edu-Ham Program for Schools and Families
The Gilder Lehrman Institute of American History
https://tinyurl.com/Edu-Ham

Graham Windham Caring for Kids & Families
(The New York Orphan Asylum Society, co-founded by Eliza Hamilton in 1806) www.graham-windham.org; info@graham-windham.org

The Alexander Hamilton Awareness Society:
(The AHA Society) www.theAHASociety.org

Museum of American Finance:
www.moaf.org

The Society of the Cincinnati:
societyofthecincinnati.org

Mary Anne's Talk at the Nevis Tea party: 1-11-18
https://tinyurl.com/MAH-NevisTea-1-11-18

Channel 8 video-Mary Anne @ Coast Guard Statue: 10-12-18
https://tinyurl.com/CGAStatue

Rand and Mary Anne @ Seminole Historical Society: 6-23-19
https://tinyurl.com/MAHSeminoleHistorical

Mary Anne-Nevis Statue Unveiling Video Greetings: 7-22-22
https://tinyurl.com/MAH-7-22-22

Video of *Moving The Hamilton Grange*: 6-7-08
https://tinyurl.com/movingthegrange

**The First Annual Alexander Hamilton Lecture delivered by
The Honorable Laurens M. Hamilton: January 7, 1966.**
https://tinyurl.com/LaurensHamiltonSpeech

Mary Anne at the Seminole Library Author Fair: 11-4-23
https://tinyurl.com/SeminoleLibraryPresentation

Mary Anne's International Radio Interview by Donna Seebo: 11-8-23
https://tinyurl.com/MaryAnnesInterview

APPENDIX II
Additional Historical Details

Page 45 Omni Homestead Resort Warm Springs and Hot Springs, Virginia. In 1965, Laurens took our family on a Pullman train to this resort in Hot Springs, Virginia for Christmas. The Warm Springs, where Alexander Hamilton was once a guest, were about 5 miles north but the area closed in the 1920s. J. P. Morgan helped raise funds for the resort in the 1890s. In the 1950s, a new development, the snow gun, was used to convert an old golf course into a ski slope. An Olympic-size ice rink was built, too. Thus, the resort was able to expand from seasonal to year-round. The railroad was abandoned in 1970.

Source: The Homestead and Warm Springs Valley, Virginia, by Stan Cohen ISBN13: 978-1-891852-07-7. June, 1984

Page 51 J. P. Morgan The first president of the Metropolitan Club of New York was J. P. Morgan, elected in February, 1891. Born into a banking family, he eventually branched out to build businesses in steel, railroads, and even electricity. His house and office were two of the first to be electrified by his friend, Thomas Edison. Others signed on for electricity, but not one prominent family who provided oil for lamps. In addition to funding inventions, Mr. Morgan used his resources to stabilize the federal economy during difficult times.

Source: https://guides.loc.gov/this-month-in-business-history/april/jp-morgan-born

Page 156 Mepkin Abbey This quiet, serene, and peaceful plantation has gorgeous gardens and is home to a Trappist monastery. Located near Charleston, South Carolina, the site includes several miles of Cooper River frontage and 3,000 acres of beautifully preserved and maintained woodland and farmland.

Source: mepkinabbey.org

Page 157 David Downey, a friend who joined us in Nevis, is a USMC veteran who is also active in the Coast Guard. In 1942, his cousin was on board the **USCGC *Hamilton* WPG-34,** which was torpedoed by the Germans at the start of WWII near Iceland.

Dave's cousin died in that fatal attack. The vessel was located in 2011. In 2013, a dive team successfully attached a memorial plaque to the ship, honoring all who died.
Source: theahasociety.org/uscg-cutter-alexander-hamilton-wpg-34/
For more information: www.tinyurl.com/CGCutter-Hamilton-34-Iceland

Page 158 The Society of the Cincinnati Diamond Eagle - After her husband died in 1799, Martha Washington sent the Diamond Eagle to Alexander Hamilton, the Society's second president. After Hamilton died in 1804, Eliza gave it to the next president, Charles Pinckney, who formally transferred the Diamond Eagle to the Society in 1811. All subsequent presidents have worn it.
Source: https://www.societyofthecincinnati.org/the-society-of-the-cincinnati-eagle/

Page 159-1 After clearing security protocols, we attended a speech and took a tour of the **US Treasury Building.** We saw the Cash Room, the Chase Suite, and the Andrew Johnson Suite, his temporary White House office immediately following Lincoln's assassination in 1865.
Source: https://home.treasury.gov/about/history/the-treasury-building

Page 159-2 Rand drove me to the Philadelphia Historic District. We met for lunch with fellow *AHA Society* members at **City Tavern,** where the Founding Fathers met to strategize before their meetings. Unfortunately, the eatery closed in 2020 due to the pandemic. The National Park Service may seek another vendor.
Source: https://www.nps.gov/inde/planyourvisit/citytavern.htm

Page 159-3 The National Park Service opened the **First Bank of the United States** for us to see. As the first Secretary of the Treasury, Hamilton requested central banking so the economy could grow. Jefferson said the bank was not in the Constitution, argued with Hamilton, and even after the measure passed, he lobbied to have the president veto it. President Washington gave Hamilton a week to come up with his rebuttal. Hamilton delivered a 15,000-word argument and swayed Washington. The First Bank opened in a temporary location in 1791.
Source: https://www.nps.gov/inde/learn/historyculture/places-firstbank.htm

Page 159-4 We attended the six-part **Hamilton-Was-Here** set of interactive exhibits. Hosted at the American Revolution Museum, the event offered "hands-on" experiences based on Hamilton's military and government roles.
Source: https://www.amrevmuseum.org/exhibits/hamilton-was-here-rising-up-in-revolutionary-philadelphia

Page 159-5 Rand pushed me in a wheel chair as we revisited the Philadelphia Historic District. At **Independence Hall** we saw the **Liberty Bell**, descriptive exhibits, and a film.
More Information: https://www.nps.gov/inde/learn/historyculture/stories-libertybell.htm

Page 159-6 Rand gave a speech at the **Washington Crossing on the Delaware River Park**, and another speech nearby the next evening. Many reenactments occur at this site around Christmas, the day the original daring feat succeeded. Before we left New Jersey, we stopped in Princeton to view **Aaron Burr's grave**. It was drizzling rain and Rand may have been a little punchy taking pictures.
More Information: https://www.washingtoncrossingpark.org/cross-with-us/myths/

Page 160-1 In Morristown, New Jersey, we stopped to view the **Ford Mansion,** which General George Washington used as winter headquarters during the Revolutionary War. For the 6-month duration, the family lived in two rooms while the dignitaries took over the rest of the house.
Source: https://www.nps.gov/morr/learn/historyculture/ford-mansion-washington-s-headquarters.htm

Page 160-2 Down the road we visited the **Thomas Paine Monument.** The statue shows Paine in 1776, using a drum as a table during the withdrawal of the army across New Jersey, while composing the first of the *Crisis Papers.*
Source: http://thomas-paine-friends.org/historical-places.htm

Page 160-3 The **Jabez Campfield House** is also known as the **Schuyler-Hamilton House**, where a young Alexander courted Eliza. In 1923, just before it was to be destroyed, it was purchased by the Daughters of the American Revolution and now serves as the chapter headquarters.
Source: https://morristownnjdar.org/history-of-the-schuyler-hamilton-house/

Page 160-4 **Table Rock Estate** Italian masons were imported to build the grand estate. Construction of the 2,000-acre Table Rock Estate began around 1900 and the cornerstone was laid in 1904. All stones were quarried on the property. The largest room, the Ballroom, measured 83 by 22 feet and featured a giant fireplace at one end. Laurens recalled that up to 75 servants were employed when he lived there. In the early 40s, the Sister Servants of Mary Immaculate bought the buildings and multiple acres.

More information: https://ssmi-us.org/about-us/the-sloatsburg-estate/

Page 163-1 We visited the **Dey Mansion**, built by Dirck Dey and his son, Theunis. During the Revolution, Theunis, commanded the Bergen County Militia. Colonel Dey offered the easterly side of the house to General Washington when the commander-in-chief used it for his headquarters in July, October and November of 1780.

Source: https://www.americanheritage.com/content/dey-mansion-washingtons-headquarters

Page 163-2/3 On the evening of Friday the 13th, 2018, Rand and I went to **Bar SixtyFive.** Perched 65 floors above Rockefeller Center, this is the highest outdoor terrace bar in New York City. The headwaiter took us into the **Rainbow Room**, where Laurens had taken me to see the view, dance, and listen to the music fifty-two years ago. Both venues are now closed, except for special rental parties and events.

Source: https://www.therooftopguide.com/rooftop-bars-in-new-york/bar-sixtyfive-at-rainbow-room.html

Page 163-4 Saturday morning, we went to see the **Morris-Jumel Mansion** in Washington Heights. Built in1765 as a summer residence for British Colonel Roger Morris, his wife, Mary, and their family, they abandoned it prior to the Revolutionary War due to increasing tensions. General Washington, who had fought with Colonel Morris as allies in a prior war, used the abandoned building as his field headquarters. The mansion was confiscated and sold after Mary was accused of treason. Stephen and Eliza Jumel bought it in 1810. Stephen died in 1832. In 1833, Eliza married her second husband, the former Vice-President Aaron Burr, in the home's front parlor. Eliza Jumel filed for divorce four months after the marriage, and hired Alexander Hamilton, Jr. as one of her divorce attorneys. Burr died in a Staten Island rooming house the day the divorce was to be finalized in 1836.

Source: https://morrisjumel.org/stories/history-of-the-house/

Page 165-1 General Jedediah Huntington House
After Jedediah Huntington graduated from Harvard in 1763, he earned a master's degree from Yale in 1770. During the same timeframe, he was appointed ensign in the first Norwich militia in 1769 and was quickly promoted.

In the spring of 1776, as a colonel in the 20th Regiment, he marched to Boston where his unit was part of the force that occupied Dorchester Heights. After the British left, he marched back to New York, and, along the way, he planned to host a conference for General George Washington at his family home, Huntington House, in Norwich, Connecticut. But, reportedly, it was hosted at his father Jabez's house instead.

Prominent Huntington House guests include Marquis de Lafayette (1778) and painter John Trumbull (multiple visits). In 1783, Huntington served on the committee of four men who drafted the constitution of the Society of the Cincinnati. After returning to his home, he was appointed customs collector by President Washington in 1789. He continued in his position and resided at Huntington House until his death in 1818. NOTE: Huntington House is now a private residence.
Source: https://allthingsliberty.com/2018/04/jedediah-huntington-of-connecticut/

Page 165-2 In 2018, we visited **Mystic Harbor Museum**, which is home to more than 500 historic watercraft. Included are four National Historic Landmark vessels, most notably the 1841 whaleship Charles W. Morgan, America's oldest commercial ship still in existence.
Source: https://www.mysticseaport.org/

Page 165-3 We also saw the **Slater Memorial Museum**, a treasure trove of art from five continents in Norwich, CT. The Romanesque Revival-style building, designed by Worcester architect Stephen Earle and dedicated in 1886, features stained glass windows, marble mosaics, intricate pressed brick architectural details, and carved oak, chestnut and cherry moldings. It's located on the Norwich Free Academy campus, one of only two schools to have an art museum on site.
Source: https://www.norwichct.org/Facilities/Facility/Details/108

APPENDIX III
More Memorable Stories

Christmas 1964 One of my many life's challenges was during the holidays in 1964. We had filed for a divorce that summer and I worked at the Gramercy Inn, trying to make ends meet. After saving money for Christmas gifts for the children, I went shopping one day and stored the gifts in my station wagon. While I was at work, someone broke the wing window of my car and stole all the gifts. My insurance agent reimbursed me based on my receipts, but I had to rebuy all the gifts…and I HATE shopping!

Winter 1965 At times, I regretted not accepting the *free* new car Laurens ordered for me. I liked the new Pontiac I'd bought but I still had a car loan to repay. I should have considered that before I made him cancel his order.

Spring 1979 After Laurie passed away, I remembered how friendly folks in Nevis were, so I thought about selling my place and moving there. I put it on the market but it didn't sell, so I didn't move. I'm so glad I stayed.

Spring 1983 When my birth daughter, Allison, found me, I had to inform her that the hospital had put the wrong date on her birth certificate. Her son had been proud to be born on his mom's birthday, but he was actually born the day before. She didn't change the certificate but she celebrates the real date.

Page 19 A Life-long Affinity For an unknown reason, numbers and dates have always been intriguing to me, especially "4" and "8." I was born on February 4, I met Laurie on November 4, and we got married on May 4. I also met Mother Teresa on June 4. My parents were married on February 8, my divorce was finalized on February 8, and Laurie died on February 8. "2-8" is a significant date for me. A news article was published about me on May 28, 2016. The first day I saw this (proof) book was June 28, 2023.

Page 54 1966-2018 As a Hamilton advocate, I've met many wonderful people over the years who've enhanced my life. Most have some direct or indirect connection to the Hamilton family legacy. But not all.

One example involves two young local boys, who always bring back warm memories near and dear to my heart. They have absolutely nothing to do with Hamilton, except that I happened to meet them on Nevis in the '60s.

As mentioned in Chapter 5, Floris and his brother played on the beach with us, rode a donkey, and took us to Mass during my first Nevis trip in 1966.

During another visit, 17 years later, I asked the Hamilton Museum staff about the boys. Floris was in his mid-20s and came to visit me at the museum. The next time I saw him, decades later, he was in his early 50s.

Floris and his brother took us to Mass in 1966. He visited me in 1983 (left) and in 2018.

You may wonder how the staff found him after so many years. The island is so small that everyone knows everyone. This is one of my fondest memories I cherish about my numerous Hamilton advocate adventures.

Photos by Vince Post, Jr.

Page 95 In 1980, I missed Rainbow but got **Rainboe** vanity plates which are still mounted on my **1999 Ruby Red Cadillac DeVille**, pictured above.

Page 121 1986 Nevis. My friend, Peggy, showed Betsy and me around the island. We visited **Montpelier Plantation,** where Princess Diana took her sons for a vacation in January, 1993. I enjoyed riding a horse along the beach near the Cliffdwellers Inn. We also visited Fort Charles near the Bath Hotel.

Page 157 2018. We visited the restaurant at the **Hamilton Hotel**. I had worked there in the 1950s so I showed my old picture album of that time to the current workers. Later we met a group of AHA Society members for dinner at the **Hamilton Restaurant** across from the Willard Hotel.

Page 157 *Hamilton By the Slice -* After our Hamilton Birthday call in 2018, I was in the Hamilton Museum waiting to speak at the Scholarship Tea. A small book caught my eye: *Hamilton by the Slice* by William G. Chrystal. It was the only purchase I made that trip. Upon our return home, David Downey and I drove to the Tampa Airport and picked up Rand, who was returning from New York. We went to my condo and Rand saw the book *Hamilton by the Slice* sitting on the table. He said he knew the author William (Bill) Chrystal, so he called him in Virginia and we had a delightful conversation.

Page 157 *Hamilton vs. Jefferson* **Video** - Bill Chrystal sent me a couple of tapes of him portraying Alexander Hamilton and Clay Jenkinson playing the part of Thomas Jefferson in front of college and community audiences. After their performances, they answered questions, sometimes in character. I enjoyed their shows very much.

Page 173 As of early 2023, the ownership of the lost-but-found **Dorothy Dress** from the *Wizard of Oz* is still hung up in court (no pun intended), nearly 2 years after the dress reappeared in the Catholic University drama room.

Page 175 Seeking John Wallace Hamilton's Family In the 1980s, I gave a set of 6 or 7 books by John Church Hamilton about *Alexander Hamilton,* to an attorney in St. Petersburg, Florida. His obituary was posted in 2014. If anyone has information about his family, I'd like help contacting them. If they still have the books, I'd like to confirm they know their historical value. Please email: mahmr2428@gmail.com

ARTICLE NOTES

 Arundel, Wendy, *The Strange Tale of Outer Baldonia, Maine Boats, Homes and Harbors*, March/April 2020.
Source: maineboats.com/print/issue-163/strange-tale-outer-baldonia

 Durante, Dianne, *New Alexander Hamilton Sculpture at US Coast Guard Academy,* Dianne L Durante, Writing Addict + Adept Blog, October 15, 2018.
Source: diannedurantewriter.com/archives/7478

 Meacham, Andrew, *Mary Anne Hamilton, a relative of Alexander Hamilton, gets the trip of a lifetime, Tampa Bay Times,* Tampa, Florida: May 28, 2016.
Source: https://tinyurl.com/MAH-trip-of-a-lifetime

 Seegers, Scott, *Death and the Friendly River*, Readers Digest, January, 1968
Source: https://tinyurl.com/AccidentOnTheRiver

BIBLIOGRAPHY

Brockenbrough, Martha. *Alexander Hamilton Revolutionary*. New York: Macmillan Publishing, 2017.

Chernow, Ron. *Alexander Hamilton*. New York: Penguin, 2004.

Freeman, Joanne B. *The Essential Hamilton, Letters, and Other Writings*. New York: Library of America, 2017.

Levinson, Adam. *Statues and Stories: Collections and Reflections on American Legal History*, accessed May 28, 2023. https://statutesandstories.com/index.html

McCullough, David. *1776*. New York: Simon & Schuster, 2005.

Medved, Michael. *The American Miracle, Divine Providence in the Rise of the Republic*. New York: Penguin Random House, 2016.

Miranda, Lin-Manuel, and Jeremy McCarter. *Hamilton: The Revolution*. New York: Grand Central Publishing, 2016.

Newton, Michael E. *Alexander Hamilton, The Formative Years*. Phoenix: Eleftheria Publishing, 2015.

Newton, Michael E. *Discovering Hamilton, New Discoveries in the Lives of Alexander Hamilton, His Family, Friends, and Colleagues*. Phoenix: Eleftheria Publishing, 2019.

Shiller, Sophie. *The Lost Diary of Alexander Hamilton*. Texas: Printed by the Author, 2020.

Sylla, Richard. *Hamilton: The Illustrated Biography*. New York: Union Square, 2016.

Wilser, Jeff. *Alexander Hamilton's Guide to Life*. New York: Penguin Random House, 2016.

ABOUT
THE AUTHORS:

Mary Anne Hamilton has often heard: "Your life sounds unbelievable. You should write a book." Her late husband, Laurens Morgan Hamilton, was an heir to Founding Father Alexander Hamilton and global financier, J. P. Morgan. Laurens had tried unsuccessfully for over 60 years to educate everyone about his great-great-grandfather's contributions to the USA.

After seeing *Hamilton, An American Musical*, Mary Anne realized the impact of her family's heritage. She met Rand Scholet, founder and then-president of *The Alexander Hamilton Awareness Society*. Beginning in 2017, they promoted Hamilton's incredible legacy by sharing educational presentations locally, nationally, and internationally. In 2020, Covid 19 restrictions confined her to her home and her neighborhood park. Mary Anne began writing her memories and reviewing collections from the first 86 years of her life.

Rand then suggested that Mary Anne collaborate with a fellow AHA Society member, Helena Reynolds, to create a book based on her memories and activities. In addition to entertaining, inspiring, and educating readers, this book was written to extend appreciation to Lin-Manuel Miranda for creating the ingenious production, *Hamilton, An American Musical*. He, Rand, and others helped Mary Anne continue her late husband's educational efforts to promote Alexander Hamilton's legacy.

Helena Reynolds wrote her first book decades ago in an attempt to be a work-at-home mom. Critics said her book was unmarketable and that she should tear out a few family stories to sell as articles. So she did. (Two articles.)

Subsequently, she spent the next 45 years as an assistant teacher and recreation coordinator, as well as a wife, mother, and wannabe writer. She wrote intervention plans, marketing items, memos, articles, and press releases.

For the past 40 years, Helena has been recording the life stories of her Filipino immigrant family for a memory book. She even produced a highlight video of her parents' unique, WWII, five-year, unconventional pen-pal romance, involving 17 years and 7,000 miles between them.

Recently retired, she completed the 2021 and 2022 sessions of #1 *New York Times* Bestselling Author, Karen Kingsbury's *Believe* Writing Intensives near Nashville. She also accepted the challenge of co-authoring a book for her friend, Rand Scholet, of The AHA Society. He had read and shared her family's stories with his colleagues, including their mutual friend, Mary Anne Hamilton. Although Helena is a novice, he insisted she work with Mary Anne to share her recollections in a book. Shortly afterward, Rand suddenly passed away. This project honors his request.

Helena is passionate about telling life stories, especially those involving education about Founding Father Alexander Hamilton's contributions to the creation, foundation, and maturation of our great nation. She is honored to help share Mary Anne's incredible lifetime memories.

BACK COVER IMAGES REFERENCE

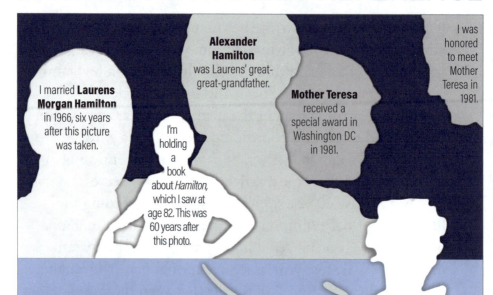

I married **Laurens Morgan Hamilton** in 1966, six years after this picture was taken.

Alexander Hamilton was Laurens' great-great-grandfather.

I'm holding a book about *Hamilton*, which I saw at age 82. This was 60 years after this photo.

Mother Teresa received a special award in Washington DC in 1981.

I was honored to meet Mother Teresa in 1981.

In 1956, my waitress uniform was a colonial-era dress. It may have—as Alexander Hamilton once wrote— "prepared the way for (my) futurity." I had no idea my future included being a Hamilton.

SPECIAL THANKS

As novice co-authors of this self-published book, we, Mary Anne Hamilton and Helena Reynolds, are publicly extending our gratitude to our graphic designer, Jason Reynolds. He was our cover creator, layout designer, and image restoration and enhancement artist. He also handled content formatting, revising, and uploading files to the publishing platform.

To contact Mary Anne Hamilton or Helena Reynolds, email: mahmr2428@gmail.com

MAHMR and Associates LLC PO Box 3278, Kent, WA 98089

Made in United States
Troutdale, OR
05/23/2025

31531789R00124